HAUNTED
PRINCE WILLIAM
COUNTY

ANDREW L. MILLS

Haunted
America

Published by Haunted America
A Division of The History Press
Charleston, SC
www.historypress.com

First published 2020

Manufactured in the United States

ISBN 9781467145534

Library of Congress Control Number: 2020938463

For the spirits of our past,
Who are never truly gone
So long as we remember…

CONTENTS

Acknowledgements	7
Introduction	9
1. Dumfries	15
Rippon Lodge	16
Weems-Botts House	22
Williams Ordinary	27
2. Occoquan	29
Occoquan Inn	30
The Shops	32
3. Haymarket	36
Snow Hill	37
Rattlesnake Grahams	37
Buckland Mills	38
La Grange	41
Thoroughfare Gap	43
Cloverland	46
4. Bristow	47
Brentsville Courthouse	47
Independent Hill	51

CONTENTS

5. Nokesville   53
    Broadlands Farm   54

6. Bull Run   56
    The Battlefield   56
    Ben Lomond   65

7. Manassas   67
    Olde Towne Inn   68
    The Things I Love   70
    Old Town Hall   70

8. Death and Society   72
    Religion and Death   72
    Gender, Fashion and Traditions   74
    Waking the Dead   76
    Picturing the Dead   78
    Containing the Dead   79
    Tombstones and Their Meanings   80
    The Lady of Death   82

9. Ghosts of a Different Kind   84

Bibliography   93
About the Author   96

ACKNOWLEDGEMENTS

As I sit in front of the computer screen finishing this book, it has become extremely important for me to think and reflect on the people who affected me while creating this text and the journey it took for me to actually sit down, begin typing and make all of this into a reality. The story behind it is rather simple: I was challenged and convinced to write this particular book. It was not as easy of a task as I thought it might be. Instead, it proved to be a long and, in some respects, forgotten task that finally found its way to completion.

I was challenged to write this text namely because of my interest in telling tales, be it of the macabre or any other type, and the fact that I have spent a number of years giving guided ghost tours through Old Town Alexandria. With my own knowledge of ghosts and spinning a good tale, it seemed almost a natural fit to write a book dealing with this particular subject.

I felt challenged to write this book primarily due to one person: myself. Could I do it? Clearly, the answer is yes, since you are reading this page. Writing has been a passion of mine for some time but, sadly, one that I had to shelve to maintain other aspects of my life. We say anyone can go back to something and do it again—almost like riding a bike. Simply put, that is a lot of rubbish. It takes a great deal of effort to get back into doing something you love. Many nights were spent wanting to write but ended the same way by staring at the computer screen with nothing to show for it and coming to the sudden realization that four or five hours had passed since I last looked at the screen, and I had inadvertently dozed off while sitting on the couch.

Acknowledgements

In the end, perseverance and stubbornness paid off, and I am able to present this work to the reading public.

I would be remiss if I did not thank a few people who were influential in aiding in the writing of this book. First, I would like to thank my wife, Lilian, and our children, Jack and Grace, for their support and love as I worked on this project. My beautiful wife has always supported my writing schemes and has never lost faith in my ability to finish whatever piece I am working on. Her ability to catch my spelling or grammatical errors before I even realize them is uncanny and, to be perfectly honest, is probably a superhero power if ever there was one. My son, Jack, has always been up for an adventure, especially with ghosts. How many times he wanted to come along to get pictures of haunted locations is beyond my recollection, but his insatiable curiosity in trying to find a ghost certainly helped keep the excitement going on our trips throughout the county. Special thanks has to go to my little Grace for being such a good sport as I went to the library to get many of my source materials and introduce her to the joy of books. How many times she read the ABC and 123 books when she was a little girl are far beyond anyone's guess.

Second, I would like to thank Wellington Watts of Alexandria Colonial Tours for getting me involved in telling tales of ghosts. Always an excellent source of information on ghosts and telling a tale, Wellington proved beyond measure an outstanding sounding board for perfecting my craft in telling a tale and getting the most out of a good scare technique.

Third, I must thank the Prince William County Historic Preservation Department for providing much of my information on the county and the haunting of its historic sites. In addition, I would like to thank Prince William County resident Tammy Picon for providing source information. The books she provided proved extremely helpful in tracking down citations necessary for the final product.

Fourth, I would like to thank Kate Jenkins, Hayley Behal and the entire staff of The History Press for turning this project from a file on my computer into an actual book. Their faith and belief that the ghosts of Prince William County deserve a book all to their own helped give me the final nudge to complete this project.

Finally, I would like to thank my father, Charles Mills, for giving me the initial nudge to get typing. If he had not, then Prince William County's spiritual secrets would never have been revealed.

—Andrew Mills
August 9, 2019

INTRODUCTION

The year was 1731. The colony of Virginia was growing with new settlers from England every month. With the ever-increasing number of people coming into the colony, it was necessary for the House of Burgesses to look at creating a new county. In examining a map of the borders, the house drew a boundary line that would encompass a large tract of land that would one day be referred to as Northern Virginia. However, before it would be known by that name, this large parcel of land would go by a different name: Prince William County.

Named after the son of King George II, the county would be centered between the two future large population centers of Manassas and Occoquan/Woodbridge. Over time, the boundaries of the county would shrink to where they currently stand. While Prince William County has been primarily a rural county, it has recently seen a dramatic change in its landscape as more people begin to move farther away from the densely populated areas of the Washington, D.C. suburbs and seek new homes. With the building of these new homes, ground that had been left undisturbed for generations was broken, and the secrets of its past began to come out into the light of day.

What kind of secrets did a rural county have to hide? The answer to that question is surprisingly answered by the very same question with a slight modification. What kind of secrets *could* a rural county have to hide?

During the 1930s and 1940s, the Federal Writers' Project hired authors to go out across the nation to write about iconic American stories. Virginians would respond to the inquiries from these authors by not only telling them about the historical events in their county but also by filling in the gaps with ghost stories to show how the past was still present in their day-to-day lives. Ironically, the people of Virginia during the Great Depression saw these ghost stories as not only appropriate but also desirable parts of historic properties. In total, over forty stories were deemed historically significant by the researchers. What made these stories so unique, though, is that they were not overly scary or gory. Instead, the stories were found to be rather tame and helped explain the idiosyncrasies of unexplainable events that occurred in the past and how people in the community came to accept these events as just how it is.

In examining Prince William County, the belief that it could not be haunted has been proven to be completely false. The county is filled with ghosts aplenty. Some relive their final moments and even appear for people. Other spirits come out and are caught on film or on video at just the right moment in time. There are both male and female spirits who haunt the county. On occasion, some spirits provide a bit of comedy, but many, depending greatly on who tells the tale, leave you with a chill running down your spine. What causes these ghosts to remain? Parapsychologists argue that ghosts remain in a location due to a sudden or tragic death. If this is the case, then Prince William County has plenty of opportunities and locations to lend credence to this belief.

So, how did the haunting of Prince William County begin? The answer is found in the beginning of Virginia itself. In 1607, Jamestown was founded, and the first permanent English colony was established in the New World. The most notable name to come out of this colony was that of Captain John Smith. Every schoolchild in the nation has heard his tale of meeting Pocahontas and the relationship they developed. It was the meeting of these two worlds that led to the creation of a spirit world bond in the land that would later be known as Prince William County.

The first mysterious event to occur to Smith and Jamestown happened when a flock of ravens, often referred to as a murder, descended on the colony and remained for some time. The significance of their arrival is that this was during the infamous Starving Time for the colony, when half the population of Jamestown died due to starvation. The ravens remained in Jamestown for a brief period of time but eventually left. Smith noted that he had never seen anything like it before. Could it have been a vision of things to come? For the starving survivors of the colony who lived to see 1608, their answer could have been yes.

Captain John Smith, who made the first contact with Native Americans in Virginia and learned about the earliest ghost stories around what would be Prince William County. *Library of Congress.*

Their sense of doom was only compounded by the sightings of indigenous people near the colony. For most Europeans, sightings of people who did not look like them were confined to tales of Moors, Vikings or the Golden Horde. The people discovered in the New World were different, and the Europeans thought they were human monsters coming to torment the fledgling colony.

The natives were described as having their skin painted from head to toe, while wearing on their heads the skins of snakes and other animals. The ceremonies they performed were unknown and unsettling to the Europeans, who watched them from afar. The early explorers of Virginia tried to describe what they saw to their fellow countrymen by likening the scenes to nightmares.

As Captain Smith moved farther and farther away from Jamestown, he began to hear tales of the supernatural from the local tribes. One tale was told to him by a native chief who said two children were viciously killed by their parents for no reason. After realizing what they had done, the parents were sorrowful and would visit the bodies of their deceased children daily. One day, they returned to the bodies and claimed that the spirits of the children had returned to them. Hearing of this miracle, other members of the tribe came to view the two resurrected children. Soon the entire tribe came to gaze on them, but their curiosity proved to be their undoing. Shortly after seeing the two, the entire village became ill with a plague that no one had seen before. Sadly, no one in the village survived.

During his exploration of the Potomac, Smith would learn of a tale that had been retold numerous times in numerous ways. The story is still a popular one to be told on the Potomac River by tour cruises. It is the curse of the three sisters. Smith claimed that he heard the sounds of moans, sobs and other cries when he passed close to the location where the story happened. When he asked for the origins of the tale, he was told an amazing story.

It had occurred at least a century before the Europeans arrived, if not earlier. At one time, tribes lived on either side of the Potomac River and warred against one another for control of the river and the power that it

The earliest map of Virginia, created by Captain John Smith, which shows the Potomac River leading toward where Prince William County would be created. *Library of Congress.*

had. Living in one of the villages on the Maryland side of the river was a medicine man who was wicked and cruel when wielding his magic. The medicine man had three daughters who were both kind and beautiful.

The three daughters fell in love with three warriors in the village but had to keep their love secret from their father because he would not have approved of them. One day, the warriors crossed the river in search of food and were captured by an enemy village. The three men were beaten, tortured, killed and scalped. Watching from the other side of the river were the three sisters. While they were kind and beautiful, inside each of them remained dormant a monster of hatred that could only be awoken when provoked.

Witnessing the deaths of the men they loved was more than enough for the three women to bear. The monster in each of them was awoken, and they plotted their revenge. They would cross the river and find the enemy braves who killed their loves and exact the same kind of death on them—but with an added twist. They would use the magic of their father to curse those men as they begged for either mercy or death and ensure that their souls

Rock formations like these can be found throughout the Potomac River. *Author's collection.*

would be tormented forever by pain and agony. With their plan set, the three sisters began to put it into motion.

The sisters got their hands on a raft and proceeded to cross the Potomac River. As they did so, a storm came across the area, making the river impossible to cross. The sisters were unable to get back to their side. Realizing that they would never be able to get back to land, they shouted out a curse saying that if they could not cross the river at this spot, then no one could. With that, they jumped into the river and drowned. As they drowned, the sky darkened and lightning seared into the river where the three had died, forming three rocks that are now known as Three Sisters Rocks.

To date, anyone who has tried to cross the Potomac River by those rocks has drowned. Attempts to build bridges across that particular part of the river have also been met with challenges, as any construction site that is created winds up destroyed by a force of nature. If a massive storm comes through and the sounds of sobbing can be heard by the river during the storm, it means that someone will drown there soon.

With that, a haunted Prince William County began. Where John Smith heard this particular tale is debatable, but it left a mark on the region. Anyone traveling into Virginia would now know that as soon as they crossed the Potomac River, they would find themselves falling under the watchful eyes of those long-departed souls who once lived on the land on which they now decided to tread.

By looking into the haunted past of Prince William County, a person takes a journey not only into the macabre but also into the lives of those who lived here and found tragic endings not necessarily of their own making. As you read each story, it is important to understand that there will always be people who believe in ghosts and those who do not. Although this book is not designed to convince people of the existence of something supernatural, it is the hope of this author to make people open to the prospect of something else out there that we cannot otherwise see but could conceivably say is there. With that thought in mind, let us now step through the looking glass and into the haunted world of Prince William County. Some of the stories you will read will amaze you, while others might make your skin tingle or feel chill. One way or another, once you start reading, you will find yourself under their eyes, watching you, coming ever so close, until finally you hear that *thump*...made you look.

1
DUMFRIES

Nestled between Woodbridge and Stafford is the small community of Dumfries, Virginia. Many people who see the name are quick to pronounce it as "dumb fries," but there is more to the community than a comical mispronunciation of its name. The first settlers to the area came in 1690, with the founding of a gristmill. As the next generation came into its own, a sizeable population had come to the region, and there were plenty of reasons to form a town. After a great deal of political maneuvering, Dumfries would become the first and oldest town in Virginia on May 11, 1749.

The new town was named after Dumfries, Scotland. This particular name was chosen to honor the home of John Graham, whose land was used to create the town. During the next fifteen years, Dumfries would continue to grow and become more important by the minute. Its commercial trade was so great it rivaled both Boston and Philadelphia. Tobacco was the cash crop for the port town as western farmers sent their goods eastward. By 1763, Dumfries was gaining speed and appeared to be on the verge of becoming a large economic powerhouse, possibly moving its way up from being a simple town into a city. Its population and size already surpassed that of New York City.

Sadly, Dumfries peaked too soon and started to make its downward spiral almost as fast as it made its upward one. Commercial crop trade was the largest of the factors to create the town's downturn. To compete with the larger port cities, farmers cultivated the soil to the point of sheer exhaustion, eroding the soil and forcing it to slide into the Potomac River and tributary creeks. As a result, the waterline was pushed back from its original shores, and the larger ships that were used for trade could no longer reach Dumfries. Adding to this initial complication was the American Revolution. Since trade with Great Britain was suspended for almost a decade, business contracts that had otherwise been promising were now gone.

Throughout the nineteenth century, Dumfries had tried in vain to rebuild its former trade prominence by building canals that would bring shipping into the town. However, every attempt to succeed in this venture failed. By 1915, the town was declared by the *Washington Star* a "ruin." The construction of Route 1 and the creation of the marine base in Quantico would help revive some life, but this proved short-lived as rival towns like Triangle were formed and drew both people and businesses away from Dumfries.

With the hopes and dreams of those from the past who saw Dumfries as a bustling metropolis now gone, it seemed as if this small community might spend the rest of its existence in obscurity. However, it is in this obscurity that surprises can come around the corner and simply say *boo*.

RIPPON LODGE

With an early structure built in the 1720s by Richard Blackburn, Rippon Lodge would become the center of the Blackburn family's estate in Prince William County. Richard, being the family patriarch, named the home after the town of his birthplace, Rippon, England. Richard would gain wealth in his lifetime and even aided in the expansion of Mount Vernon when it was under the ownership of Lawrence Washington. When Richard Blackburn passed away, ownership of the lodge passed to his second son, Thomas.

Colonel Thomas Blackburn served as an aide to George Washington during the American Revolution and was wounded at the Battle of Germantown. He returned home from the war and continued to work to help fund the American cause on the homefront. After the war, Thomas Blackburn worked to improve economic conditions in Prince William County with the development of a road to connect Dumfries with Occoquan and Fairfax County.

As time went on, different families moved into the home and lived there from time to time. However, it would be in the early twentieth century that the first stories of ghosts on the premises began to emerge. While no one is

Left: Colonel Thomas Blackburn. *Prince William County Historic Preservation.*

Below: Rippon Lodge. *Library of Congress.*

sure what sparked the interest of ghost stories at Rippon Lodge, the oldest of these ghostly tales comes from a duel.

Around 1762, Sarah Scott was accused of striking an enslaved boy so hard that the child died. An investigation was conducted by Henry Lee, a justice of the peace in Prince William County, and Sarah was found not guilty of murder. John Baylis, who was also a justice of the peace, claimed the investigation was fraudulent because the Scott family used their influence in Prince William County to get the verdict to go in their favor.

Bad blood between the Scott family and the Baylis family grew until 1765. In that year, John Baylis and Cuthbert Bullitt fought a duel after

The entrance of Rippon Lodge is where it is believed John Baylis died after his duel with Cuthbert Bullitt. *Author's collection.*

tensions finally boiled over and there was no other means of bringing this family feud to a close. The rules for a duel are not universal, which can create tense situations. In this particular circumstance, Baylis felt that his chances of survival were better met if he tried to plead for mercy. His pleas seemed to have been met, as Bullitt hesitated to fire on his opponent after mercy was requested.

The momentary pause for compassion soon turned into treachery as Baylis pointed his pistol at his opponent and attempted to kill him in cold blood. Luckily for Bullitt, the shot missed. With the element of surprise no longer on John Baylis's side, Bullitt was given the opportunity to fire his shot. Unlike Baylis, Bullitt did not miss. Instead of getting the desired kill shot, Bullitt got the next best thing by wounding Baylis in the groin. Baylis was dragged back to Rippon Lodge, where he died from blood loss. Following his death, people reported hearing the sounds of a body being dragged across the floor, the moans of a person who was in great pain and bloodstains on the floor near the entrance of the home.

Another story that emerged from Rippon Lodge involves Mrs. Christian Scott Blackburn. As the story goes, a slave child had gotten in the way of her mistress, and the two collided in the home. Mrs. Blackburn, being outraged that such an event would ever happen to her, shoved the child away. Not realizing the strength behind the shove, Mrs. Blackburn watched as the child fell back and hit the jamb of the fireplace. The child died from the head wound, and the news of this event did not seem to faze Mrs. Blackburn in the least, even after an inquiry was called. After a careful investigation, the inquiry officially declared the incident an accident.

Later, after the death of Mrs. Blackburn, people claimed that shadows could be seen moving from the windows of Rippon Lodge, and voices were heard inside the house. It was even reported that the spot on the jamb of

Left: Mrs. Christian Scott Blackburn. *Prince William County Historic Preservation.*

Right: The fireplace jamb pictured here is where it is believed that Mrs. Blackburn injured the small slave child who later died from the injury. *Library of Congress.*

the fireplace where the child hit her head still showed blood after so many years. Others have claimed to see a little girl run toward the woods and the cemetery at Rippon Lodge.

Throughout the nineteenth century, rumors and other stories about supposed hauntings at Rippon Lodge began to arise. During a period of abandonment, two campers wandered onto the Rippon property and gained access to the home to have a comfortable place to sleep. During their impromptu stay, the two campers claimed to have heard unearthly laughter coming from inside the home.

How could these persistent stories of a haunted house in Prince William County find such longevity in local minds? The culprit behind the propagation of these stories is believed to be Judge Wade Hampton Ellis, who purchased the home in 1924 and worked to restore it for almost twenty-five years. Known as an eccentric, Ellis may have been influenced to exaggerate the stories about Rippon Lodge after reading an article from the *Manassas Journal* written in 1911. According to the article, Rippon Lodge was said to "be haunted in ghostly and sinister

Judge Wade Ellis and Mrs. Ellis. *Prince William County Historic Preservation.*

fashion that no one will occupy it, and the public road has changed its course to avoid the neighborhood."

Rippon Lodge is no longer a private home, and there are those in Prince William County who do not believe the house is haunted. These individuals try to explain the mysterious events through logic and reason. However, the belief in Rippon Lodge's ghostly past is difficult to overcome for some people.

Brendon Hanafin, director of Prince William County Historic Preservation, disagrees with the naysayers and said, "I do not like to go in there at night by myself." Stories of ghosts haunting the house from both current and former staff members include three children who like to laugh in the house and have even been captured in photographs. They have been described as small, thin, white children who must not have been eating a great deal when they were alive.

Former manager of Rippon Lodge Rebecca Super said she had never seen or heard anything but did remark that a number of the staff would make a note of saying goodnight to Mrs. Christian Blackburn before leaving. The gardener of the house was once working on the flowerbed in front of the house when she heard tapping on the window and the doorknob trying to turn. This continued until the gardener got out of the flowerbed. She felt certain that it was the spirit of Mrs. Blackburn because the former mistress of the house was notorious for making sure no one made changes to her home without her permission.

Recent hauntings of Rippon Lodge include an incident in which the house security alarm went off in the middle of the night. When park security came to the house to determine the cause of the alarm, the officer discovered that the front door was wide open. Suspecting someone was inside, the officer proceeded toward the house but distinctly heard the sound of voices directly behind him. According to the officer, the voices sounded as though they were having a party on the property. After securing the house, the officer discussed the events with the staff at Rippon Lodge. As one member of the staff explained, someone would have needed to open the front door because it was both heavy and known to stick to the door frame. In addition, Rippon Lodge had been known as a party hot spot during Prohibition. Does this mean the good times never stopped at Rippon?

However, the newest spirit to haunt Rippon Lodge is that of former caretaker Edward Hawkins. Hired during the 1920s by Judge Ellis, Hawkins was a man who silently suffered from depression in a time when many people did not notice the warning signs of the psychological disorder. Hawkins's admiration of Judge Ellis was so great that the caretaker even named his own son after his employer. After Judge Ellis passed away, Hawkins became distressed when he learned that the judge's widow planned to sell the property. Even worse for Hawkins, Mrs. Ellis had no choice but to let him go as caretaker of the property. Hawkins became depressed when he learned that he was going to lose the job he loved. Feeling that there was nothing left for him to do, Hawkins went to the chicken coop and hanged himself.

Hawkins's family remarked after his death that had it been Mrs. Ellis who died first, and the judge was still alive, then Hawkins would have been kept on in his job until the caretaker passed away. As tragic as the death was, his spirit still has a great love for the property. According to staff who work at Rippon, the spirit of Edward Hawkins has been known to interfere with any changes being made to the property that he does not like. In addition, items in the household have been known to move randomly without any of the staff knowing why they are being rearranged.

WEEMS-BOTTS HOUSE

For anyone who drives south on Interstate 95 on the way toward Richmond, depending on the time of year, by the time you get to Dale City, there might be a traffic jam, and your once-happy speed of sixty miles per hour turns into a sluggish five miles per hour—if you are lucky. As you ponder the decision to somehow get off of the highway, you'll notice a brown sign that indicates an attraction called the Weems-Botts Museum. Most visitors have no idea what this means and will pass by without a second thought.

Others, however, might take the traffic jam as an opportunity to pull out their smartphone and do a quick Google search. (Please do not do this while driving. The accident that will follow is often what causes the traffic jams on the highway.) Once done, the driver might be intrigued to check out the museum.

The Weems-Botts Museum is part of a house that had two famous owners. The first was Parson Locke Weems, who is credited with writing the first biography on the life of George Washington. This biography has become part of the national mindset of virtually everyone in the country due to two of its most memorable stories. The first is the famed tale of Washington cutting down the cherry tree. The second is the tale of Washington throwing a stone across the Potomac River. Both tales resonate in the imaginations of children and make them admire one of the nation's founding fathers.

Sadly, it takes many years for people to learn that the famous stories written by Parson Weems really are just that—stories. Weems created the cherry tree story hoping to encourage people in the nation to become more moral. If George Washington could not tell a lie, then it stood to chance that everyone else could do the same thing. As for throwing a stone across the Potomac River, the laws of physics prove that this feat is next to impossible.

Weems-Botts House. *Author's collection.*

In 1802, the house changed hands and became the property of Benjamin Botts. Botts rose to notoriety and fame as a defense attorney for Aaron Burr during his treason trial. The house was used as a law office until 1811, when Botts died in a tragic theater fire in Richmond, Virginia.

After many years, the house eventually found a new family. Richard and Annie Merchant moved into the home in 1869. The house was expanded with additional rooms and additional people—their children, Mamie and Violet. Most couples would be delighted with having two little girls, but the Merchants were troubled by poor Mamie. The little girl suffered from epilepsy. The cause of this condition was usually attributed to one of two explanations: the poor child was insane, or more frightening, she was possessed by spirits. As a result, Mamie was locked in her room to live a secluded and isolated life.

In 1905, Richard Merchant passed away, and a few months later, Mamie passed away too. Annie continued to live in the house but had the assistance of Violet to help ensure some type of comfort. It was a hard life for the two women, and at the age of ninety-eight, Annie Merchant passed away. Following the death of her mother, Violet continued to live in the house but became extremely reclusive. Neighbors claimed that they saw her through the windows, usually weeping. Anyone who had the opportunity to speak with her had been warned by Annie to not come into the house because it was haunted. The children in the neighborhood believed her and so did their parents. In 1967, Violet left the house and died a year later in a nursing home.

The house was almost demolished in 1974, when a crew was called in. Mercifully, the Town of Dumfries came to the rescue, as the Weems-Botts House was the last of the colonial homes still standing in the town. Once the house was saved, the process of restoring it was underway.

Curators for the new museum began to look at the house and consider how they could maximize its space. The first notable change was the construction of a bookcase, which was used to close off a passageway. As soon as it went up, the first official haunting of the house occurred.

According to Debbie Ward, a historical interpreter for the museum, books began to fly off of the shelves. For the average person, this statement is usually understood in a figurative manner. Ward pointed out, though, that this was less figurative and more literal, as she and other staff members saw the books go from the shelf to halfway across the room. It seemed someone or something did not like the bookshelf. Almost as fast as it went up, the bookshelf came down, and that particular spot no longer had any ghostly occurrences.

The majority of ghostly events occurred on the second story of the house in the bedroom of Mamie Merchant. Due to the number of ghostly tales that have been associated with the room, docents who guide visitors through the house do not like to mention the stories unless they are asked, and even then, it has to be for serious reasons and not foolhardy ones.

Staff members of the museum have said they have heard many sounds coming from Mamie's bedroom. These sounds range from simple footsteps to laughing to screaming. Each time these sounds are heard, the staff runs up to the room to discover that it is empty.

As tours began and people were entering into the home, one of the most common comments expressed by visitors was a sense of discomfort and pressure, almost like claustrophobia. The most amazing spiritual story came from a Boy Scout troop that visited the house. A staff member noticed that the troop leader appeared to be disoriented and might be feeling unwell. When asked, the leader responded with a chill declaration. He informed the staff member that a woman wanted to know where her rocking chair was. After describing what the woman looked like, the museum staff member was stunned to discover that the description provided by the scout leader was an exact description of Mamie Merchant.

Even more astounding was a discovery made shortly after the incident occurred. The museum reached out to remaining distant relatives of the Merchant family who might have known Mamie and Violet. During a phone conversation with some of the distant relatives, the staff learned that there was a rocking chair in Mamie's room that she loved to sit and rock in.

Even with the search for the rocking chair, there are signs that Mamie has been up to something in her room. The closet door is known to mysteriously open. Staff members have repeatedly closed the door, and each time they return to the room, the door has been opened once more. On one occasion, a staff member came in and discovered something strangely different about the room. The bed inside Mamie's room appeared to have had the impression of a person who had spent time on it. While it might seem possible that a tourist opted to sit down on the bed for a quick camera pose, there is a little-known fact about the bed that only the staff knew. The bed is extremely weak. The slat underneath it that holds up the mattress is cracked, and any substantial weight placed on it would cause the entire bed to crash to the floor. This impression left on the bed showed that someone or something had been able to successfully put weight on the bed without making it break.

On the whole, everyone who currently or previously worked for the museum generally agrees that the house is haunted by spiritual dwellers. Even though the spirit of Mamie is almost a certainty, there has been discussion among some of the employees that the spirit of Violet Merchant still wanders through the house. Part of the reasoning behind this comes from the fact that the house is unexplainably cold. Even during the summertime, the internal temperature of the house is much cooler than it ought to be. The staff has its own theories about why the temperature is so icy cold. Staff members believe that this is because the lives of both Mamie and Violet were rather sad, and their spirits continue their sad existence in the house, draining the warmth of happiness that is otherwise around them.

The haunting of this house became so well known that it was described as the fourth-most-active haunted house in Virginia. In 2017, the Travel Channel sent a television crew from the show *The Dead Files* to examine the house and learn about the spirits. Investigator Amy Allan claimed to have encountered a female spirit who desired to hurt the living. While this investigation was not the first, it certainly proved to be very eventful.

Another investigation conducted five years earlier found *Potomac Local* reporter Stephanie Tipple examining the legitimacy of the haunting of the Weems-Botts House. Stephanie admitted that she did lean toward being a believer and certainly had her views confirmed when she felt the warmth and pressure of human touch on her body despite no one actually being there. Added to this were recordings of voices from multiple spirits in the building. With these incidents, Stephanie admitted that there is something at the Weems-Botts House.

Merchant Park, where wounded Union soldiers were treated and, in some cases, died. *Author's collection.*

If recordings in the house show that there are multiple ghosts in its walls, then who could they be? The answer could come from a source quite literally closer to the home than people might realize. As visitors come to the Weems-Botts House, they learn about the history of the building, and if their excitement about ghosts is satisfied with the tales of Mamie and Violet, then they sometimes find themselves treated to an extra tidbit. Merchant Park, where the house is located, is also haunted. During the Civil War, the park was used by Union medics as a triage center. For many who were wounded during the war, triage was almost tantamount to death, as infections were quick to set in and simply getting drunk while you bled to death was preferable to letting the surgeons get their hands on you.

In 1997, visitors were walking along, and a child saw a person in uniform walking along the grounds of the park. When the child returned to the visitor center and saw a postcard of some soldiers, the youngster pointed to one and said that was the person he saw. The staff at the visitor center knew there were not any reenactments going on that day or at any other time on the grounds and felt chills at realizing the ghosts of the Weems-Botts House were no longer alone but were now roaming the grounds outside of the building.

WILLIAMS ORDINARY

When driving down Route 1 toward Stafford, Virginia, you will pass a few buildings in Dumfries, and you will probably not even notice all of them. One of the buildings that can be overlooked is a colonial structure known as Williams Ordinary. Williams Ordinary proves to be a great mystery in and of itself. No one has been able to definitively place a date on its construction or completion, and nobody knows who actually built it. Records indicate that the building was in existence since at least 1798, but historians have argued that the building was built sometime between 1758 and 1765. The builder is believed to have been James Wren, who was also responsible for building Christ Church in Alexandria and other buildings throughout Northern Virginia. The building was used as an inn, tavern and hospital. Today, it is the home of Prince William County's historic preservation department.

Although the county employees who work in the building have not made any comments about the structure being haunted, previous owners and travelers who have spent the night there have said that there are ghosts residing in the building.

Williams Ordinary when it was used as a lodging establishment. *Library of Congress.*

Williams Ordinary is currently the home of the Prince William County Historic Preservation Division. *Author's collection.*

The most adamant person to describe these events was Peter Costello, who owned the Ordinary in 1985. Costello said that when he first bought the Ordinary, it seemed to him as though something in the house did not want him living there. As he worked on the structure, he heard the sounds of people moving around the house. When he called out to them, the movement continued for a few minutes and then stopped. He went to investigate who was visiting him, but no one was found. In another instance, Costello said that all of the clocks in the Ordinary stopped at 2:00 a.m. Some people could argue that a power outage will stop any clock that happens to be plugged in. This would be true under normal circumstances, but it does not explain how clocks working under battery power would do the same thing.

Even though ghosts like to play pranks and go out of their way to scare us, Costello did say that he was approached by a man who said that when the Ordinary was still being used as an inn, he spent the night there and was visited by a spirit. The man was a teenager at the time and had decided to run away from home and try to make his way in the world. The spirit walked up to his bed, stood at the foot of it and looked down at him. As the teen looked up at the spirit, the ghost spoke and warned him that he needed to be careful. What this young man had to be careful about is anyone's guess, but it seemed to do something for him. The young man took the advice of the ghost and changed his life for the better. The teenager would grow up and became a successful insurance salesman.

2

OCCOQUAN

The word *Occoquan* means "at the end of the water." It seems rather appropriate for this small Virginia town. Located near the end of the Occoquan River as it connects with the Potomac, the small, bustling town of Occoquan lives up to its reputation as "romantic beyond conception." With the small shops, little restaurants and classically designed buildings, the town provides a shopping holiday in the middle of the hustle and bustle of suburban Northern Virginia.

Like Dumfries before it, Occoquan started its existence as a location meant for trade and commerce. The greatest benefit Occoquan had was that the people who lived in the town were open to taking chances and investing in new ideas. The biggest gain for Occoquan was the production of iron through forges and mills. In the late 1700s, the town's gristmill would become the first in the nation to use a revolutionary method called the Evans System. This system automated the entire milling process, effectively lowering the size of the workforce while increasing the production capabilities of the mill. This system impressed President George Washington so much that he decided to invest in the system himself.

By 1828, Occoquan had one of the first cotton mills in Virginia and continued to thrive as a trade city for farmers in western Virginia. The waterways used by vessels trying to get to the town became too shallow for larger vessels to reach, and many expected Occoquan to suffer the same fate as Dumfries. Unlike Dumfries, Occoquan survived for two reasons. First, the town was luckily located right next to major roads for transportation, thus allowing trade goods to go by cart either north or south. Second, the people of the town provided enough charm and warm ambiance to make visitors want to stop by and enjoy the town's surroundings. Because of this second reason, visitors began to notice that the town had a peculiar set of residents who had thoughts of their own and a desire to make sure their presence was always felt.

Occoquan Inn

When looking for a place to eat in the small town, visitors will find many choices available. From seafood to trendy coffee shops and pizza restaurants to candy stores, Occoquan can indulge a person's appetite for an entire daily outing. Found in the center of the town, the Occoquan Inn is well known for many of its dishes and, more importantly, its ghost story.

In 1810, a Doeg Indian became enamored with the wife of the owner of the inn. One night as the Indian was sneaking down the stairs, the husband killed him when the two stumbled across each other. Following the Indian's death, his spirit has been said to haunt the ladies' room at the inn. When women look into the mirror, he is said to appear and look at them using the mirror. When the women turn around to confront the unwanted intruder, the Indian disappears.

Visitors to the restaurant are naturally intrigued with the story and enjoy the thrill of dining at the haunted establishment. While visiting the inn for its Sunday brunch, my assistants and I set out to learn more about the ghost. Venturing up to the second floor of the inn, we found the restrooms and began to take pictures of the area. While doing this, I took a few steps into the supposedly haunted bathroom to get a better understanding of how the story came to exist. After I took only four steps into the room, the door suddenly began to close behind me, even as one of my assistants was holding it open. According to her, the door felt as though someone else was holding it and forcing it shut on her.

My other assistant went into the men's room and quickly ran out. Paler than a proverbial ghost, he reported that the cabinet door under the sink opened on its own in front of him. Even I have to admit feeling as though there was an extra presence in the area as I looked into a mirror that was

Above, left: The staircase where the Doeg Indian who was having an affair with the innkeeper's wife was killed. *Author's collection.*

Above, right: The entrance to the restrooms at the Occoquan Inn, where my assistants and I had our own ghostly experience. *Author's collection.*

Right: The sidewalk sign for the Occoquan Inn. *Author's collection.*

centered between the two bathrooms. It felt like there was a great deal of pressure building up around my body, and it would not go away until I moved away from the mirror. Was the spirit of the Doeg Indian trying to get our attention, or was he trying to get rid of us?

The Shops

When visiting Occoquan, many people fall in love with the simple shops and craft stores that line the streets along the Occoquan River. In many ways, the small town seems to be the perfect escape from the rigors of everyday life, and it gives visitors the chance to buy some quaint, old-fashioned items to decorate their homes.

Many shopkeepers admit that their businesses have ghosts in them. For the most part, these spirits have been harmless, but they like to play the occasional prank on the shopkeepers. Merchandise will be moved, and there have been reports of footsteps being heard in some of the older buildings. In one shop, a former shopkeeper who used to live there has been known to appear in the windows, and this spirit still tries to run her own shop. The spirit is an older woman who has reportedly been known to wave a menacing finger toward people walking by who she does not like. She will even chase children from her store if they are disruptive.

Tastefully Yours, a little wine, cheese and gelato shop, boasts on its menu that it has a ghost in the building named Molly. This spirit's story begins with Molly having fallen in love with a married man. When he decided to end the relationship, Molly was heartbroken and decided to hang herself in the house where she lived. Her spirit remains in the room where she died. According to the owner of Tastefully Yours, Molly has been known to rearrange some of the wine bottles in the Brew Room, which is a tasting room at the shop.

Molly is not the only spirit who likes to rearrange merchandise at a store. According to Sandra Camp, who worked at Waterfront Antiques in 1985, there was the ghost of a woman who was referred to by the staff as Shopping Charlotte. Her spirit was closely associated with a red flapper dress from the 1920s. While working alone one day, Sandra claimed that she moved the dress once to bring boxes into the store, but when she returned to take the dress back to where it originally was, it was already there. While Waterfront Antiques is no longer in existence today, many other shops can be found along the waterfront of Occoquan.

If history has taught us anything, it is best to be careful of what we are buying. One woman purchased a trunk while visiting Occoquan and was told by the sales lady that the piece of luggage simply gave her the creeps.

Left: The Brew Room at Tastefully Yours. *Author's collection.*

Right: 302 Occoquan Street, where Shopping Charlotte is said to haunt. *Author's collection.*

The purchaser looked it over and decided to purchase the trunk because she liked the way it looked and thought she could give it a good home. Little did she realize that she got more than she bargained for.

Returning home, she placed the trunk in a nice decorative spot inside her home and went about her daily life. When she looked at the trunk, she occasionally noticed an oddity about it. She claimed that she saw a flash of light appear in the crack between the body of the trunk and the lid. The light would move about and then streak away. Uncertain of what it was, the woman felt a chill running down her back but thought it could have been her imagination running away from her.

The strange light would have been enough to frighten anyone, but the woman discovered that the entity that came with this light also had some peculiar tastes. It was the age of tape players, and the woman enjoyed listening to country music. When she played her tapes, she noticed that the music would turn down to a point that she could not even hear it. She thought it could have been the batteries, but when she tried it with a plugged-in boom box and the low volume continued, it was enough to make her wonder if the trunk was truly haunted.

Oddly enough, her new spectral friend did have some taste in music. She claimed that the spirit enjoyed listening to the waltz and would turn the music up anytime she played that or anything else classified as classical.

In total, there are reportedly nine buildings that are haunted by ghosts in Occoquan. All of the shops have various degrees of ghostly activity, most of which involve the ghosts wanting to be more helpful than hurtful. Yet there is one particular story that may be scarier than any other ghost tale, as it is not only true but also spine tingling.

It deals with a tombstone that bears no name but is the last remaining symbol of a story worth telling. During the latter half of the nineteenth century, a common practice was to put advertisements in newspapers seeking another someone to marry. This mail-order bride system was popular in states like California, where women had the opportunity to gain more rights than in other parts of the country.

For Cecelia Nien, the opportunity to get married was presented by a local man named George Arnold. The two had been corresponding and decided to get married after meeting each other for the first time. Delighted, the two were wed and began to live together in what should have been pure happiness.

Instead, Cecelia discovered that another man, Frederick Hurlebaus, had fallen in love with her before she came to Occoquan. Frederick had come from Ohio, where Cecelia was originally from, with every intention of convincing her to leave George Arnold and marry him. Cecelia repeatedly

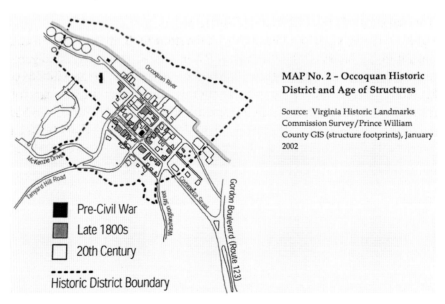

MAP No. 2 – Occoquan Historic District and Age of Structures

Source: Virginia Historic Landmarks Commission Survey/Prince William County GIS (structure footprints), January 2002

Map of Occoquan showing its historic boundaries and footprints of historic structures. Presented in town council meeting, May 19, 2015. *Author's collection.*

refused Frederick's advances. Frederick felt that he had one last option. Deciding to try the ultimate gambit, Frederick bought a ring and had a marriage license ready when he showed up at her home.

On his arrival, Frederick pleaded with Cecelia to marry him. When she denied him this time, Frederick drew out his pistol and proceed to kill himself right in front of her. This horrifying sight was only made worse when Frederick's last wishes were announced. Prior to his arrival, Frederick had built a simple coffin for himself and purchased an inscribed tombstone. He had written out that his final wish was to be buried in front of the Arnold house with his tombstone facing the building for Cecelia to see every day.

It does not appear that his final wish was actually honored, as the exact location of his burial is subject to debate in Occoquan. What is known is *where* the tombstone was located. According to local historians, Hurricane

The tombstone of Frederick Hurlebaus, located at the Mill Street Museum in Occoquan. *Author's collection.*

Agnes was so strong that it helped to pull the stone up from the riverbed and wash it to the banks of the Occoquan River where present-day Madigan's restaurant currently stands. Today, the tombstone is found in the Mill Street Museum. What is truly astounding about this stone is that it took years for town historians to identify Frederick's name on the stone. The stone also has the initials of Cecelia and the street where she lived in Ohio. Not one to let himself go without being remembered, Frederick described himself as dying from a cruel fate: love.

3

HAYMARKET

The existence of this town is owed in part to the Iroquois Nation. Before Europeans arrived in America, the location of the town was the center of the nation's hunting grounds. By the time the earliest settlers arrived, they realized its importance and began to build up the area for a future town. In 1799, the town of Haymarket was being built. With it developed the nickname of the Crossroads.

It would not be until 1852 that Haymarket would begin to grow with the arrival of the Manassas Gap Railroad. The Civil War would slow the growth of the town after Union soldiers burned all but four of the buildings. After the war, Haymarket was able to become an incorporated town in 1882.

Ten years later, the town was featured in the *Washington Post* due to mob law. Lee Heflin and Joseph Dye were convicted of murdering a girl and were sentenced to death. The local populace, feeling that the justice system was too slow, decided to take matters into their own hands by hanging the two men themselves. Oddly enough, some citizens thought that hanging might have been too good for the two criminals and decided to shoot their bodies just for good measure.

With the creation of Interstate 66, the prospects of real estate development helped bring the promise of more people to the western portions of the county. In 1994, Haymarket almost became the home of a new Disney theme park, but local resistance to the project, along with concerns over possible damages to the Manassas Battlefield, brought an end to what would have been a major economic windfall to Prince William County. The land that would have been used for the theme park was eventually sold to land developers, with the exception of 405 acres, which presently makes up Camp Snyder, a Boy Scout campsite. With all of the people moving to both the town and the region, new residents soon discovered there were some very interesting neighbors to be found in the area.

SNOW HILL

Relations between Americans and Indian tribes have always been shaky at best. For generations, a certain level of ignorance existed that allowed many Americans to think that the attacks placed on them by Indians were a result of the latter being a pack of crazed savages, instead of angry people retaliating against injustices done to their culture.

In the case of Snow Hill, this point is made true due to the materials used to build the house. Inside of the building are twelve rooms paneled in poplar wood. The wood was provided by a large tree that once stood on the spot where the house now stands. When the tree was cut down, an Indian chief protested its destruction, but his words yielded nothing. The workmen who were cutting down the tree killed the Indian and proceeded to finish the job. Once completed, they buried his body under a mound of dirt that is said to still be visible to this day.

With the home's completion, guests would marvel at the skills of the artisans who worked on the interior. Their admiration, though, would be tainted with the arrival of spiritual guests. In the cellar of the house, where the roots of the tree once extended to, the Indian chief is said to appear. People who reported seeing him have not said anything about him trying to do any harm but merely state that he appears and is not pleased with the desecration of his people's land. Many attempts have been made through Indian relics and other rituals to appease the spirit, but to date, none of them have ever succeeded.

RATTLESNAKE GRAHAMS

The Graham family can be described as any typical family in Virginia who like to quarrel with one another. This family, though, seems to take the cake in this regard. They also took to fighting with anyone who might disagree with them. This resulted in the family receiving the nickname of Rattlesnake.

The family home was known as the Shelter. It is said that the house is home to two spirits. The first is that of the family butler, who still performs his duties by opening and closing the dining room doors. The other spirit is that of one of the matriarchs of the family. Determining which woman has been difficult, but what is known about her is that she may have been the most insufferable of all the Grahams. Her reputation was so bad that when she died, no one outside of the family wanted to be part of the funeral procession. Even more humiliating was that no one would even loan a cart or animal to pull the coffin to the cemetery. After the old woman was buried, her spirit proved to be so angry that the tree she was buried next to no longer had any ivy growing on it. Instead, the ivy simply died and fell off the tree, forever infected with her toxic soul.

BUCKLAND MILLS

Created by the general assembly in 1798, Buckland Mills had high ambitions of becoming a much more notable town in Virginia than fate has allowed. Considering its colorful history, there is an argument that this town should have grown to become more prosperous than Haymarket to the north and Warrenton to the south. In 1825, the Marquis de Lafayette rode through the streets to great cheers and applause, and children threw flowers before him as he entered the town.

During the Civil War, a major cavalry battle was fought between Union (USA) and Confederate (CSA) forces on October 18 and 19, 1862. This is now referred to as the Buckland Races. General J.E.B. Stuart (CSA) moved his cavalry toward Washington, D.C., forcing General H.J. Kilpatrick (USA) to chase after him. Stuart's move was seen by the Union cavalry as a retreat, but it was in fact a tactical move to allow General Fitzhugh Lee (CSA) to come up from behind and attack Kilpatrick. This tactic would have worked if not for General George Armstrong Custer (USA), who had stayed behind to guard the rear. While the initial plan of the Confederates failed, they were victorious at the end of the day, as both Custer and Kilpatrick were forced to retreat toward Gainesville and Haymarket, respectively.

Long after the Civil War, Theodore Roosevelt rode through Buckland Mills and watered his horse on a circuitous ninety-mile trip from Washington,

Left: General J.E.B Stuart. *Right*: General H.J. Kilpatrick. *Library of Congress.*

D.C., to Warrenton. Roosevelt conducted this ride to show the United States Army the importance of physical fitness, something the army still believes in and instills in its recruits.

Although Buckland Mills has become a relative afterthought in Virginia today, it does have a haunted history of its own. Located near the intersection of Routes 29 and 15, the Graham-Odescalchi House is considered to be the most haunted home in the area. It was used by a Confederate sniper who picked off Union soldiers as they crossed the bridge over a creek.

According to Mark Joyner, who bought the house in 1999, the realtor informed him that there were reports of the house being haunted, but the noise of bumps and creaks could be explained away as an old house settling in the ground. Joyner had also been told that the previous owner had died at the house after coming home drunk and passing out on the front lawn. When the neighbors found him, they took him into the house and up to his bedroom. Later in the day, concerned neighbors checked on him and discovered that he had passed away at some point, possibly due to alcohol poisoning. Could the Confederate sniper's spirit have come back to pick off one more perceived Yankee?

Left: General Fitzhugh Lee. *Library of Congress.*

Below: General George Armstrong Custer (*left*) pictured in Warrenton, Virginia, in 1863. *Library of Congress.*

Joyner may not be able to answer that question, but he did confirm ghostly events have occurred in his home ever since he moved in and made it his own. He no longer goes to bed before 10:30 p.m. When he first moved in, Joyner heard the undeniable sounds of footsteps coming up his stairs after hearing the sound of breaking glass on the first floor. Running to see who the intruder was, Joyner was met face to face with nothing. Other people have witnessed the sounds of a person walking up the stairs, always at 10:30 p.m. Joyner has comically remarked that even though his house is haunted, the ghost is punctual.

La Grange

Today, La Grange is best known for its winery, but for a select few, it is also known for the ghosts who reside there. Originally part of the land owned by the famous Robert "King" Carter, La Grange would see many owners throughout the years. In 2005, a small group of wine enthusiasts purchased the property and became known as PWC Winery. For ten months, the winery was constructed to produce wine in Prince William County, and the 1790s mansion was heavily restored for tourists and wine enthusiasts. However, in restoring the home and preparing it for the arrival of guests, there were some unexpected visitors who decided to retake their residence on the property.

The ghost stories that come from La Grange are many, but they provide for a couple of intriguing tales. The first came in 2006, when La Grange was being renovated. A neighboring family was visiting the property to see the progress of the restoration work. As the parents went around to the back of the house to try to get inside the building, they heard the distinct sound of a piano being played. Believing their children had found a way to get inside, the parents eventually discovered a side door that gave them entry to the house. After calling out to their children, the music promptly stopped.

When they reached the front door, the parents discovered their children were still outside of the house. As the parents tried to figure out how the children were able to play a piano while still being outside, the children wanted to know where the parents had found a piano to begin with. The family conducted a search of the house and discovered there were no musical instruments. Later, the winery owners did some independent research and

Top: La Grange. *Author's collection.*

Bottom: Two glasses of wine sit atop the fireplace mantel. The red wine is for Benoni Harrison and the white wine is for his wife. *Author's collection.*

discovered there had at one time been a piano in the parlor, but Benoni Harrison had left it to his nephew after his death.

The second ghost story that comes from La Grange is that of the spirit of Benoni E. Harrison. Benoni purchased La Grange in 1827 and lived there until his death in 1869. Benoni was very wealthy but was not a very large man, though his wife was a large woman. Benoni's wife was reported to have publicly humiliated her husband by picking him up and spanking him like a child in front of guests. As a result of this incident, Benoni had an additional fireplace added into the home so that he would never have to share the same hearth with his wife. His anger was so great that he even made sure his wife would get a tombstone without any inscriptions on it.

What makes this particular ghost story fascinating is how it relates to La Grange's daily operations. On the main level of the manor house is a bar where guests can do wine tastings. In this room is a fireplace mantel where the staff will leave glasses of red and white wine. This is done to appease the ghost of Benoni and ensure nothing strange happens to guests during the day. Do you believe in taking chances? Perhaps a trip to La Grange is necessary. However, it is important to never drink from another person's glass, even if they might be a ghost. You never know what might happen.

THOROUGHFARE GAP

Toward the westward section of Prince William County, you'll begin to see the Blue Ridge Mountains. Today, many of the roads have been built up and much of the landscape has been changed to make places more accessible for vehicles.

Almost lost in the Gap is Beverly Mill, a gristmill that was originally built in 1742 by Jonathan and Nathaniel Chapman. The structure was seen as an economic commodity as it helped to send grain and flour from the Shenandoah Valley toward Alexandria. Since its creation, the mill was able to produce food for American soldiers in seven wars. Sadly, in 1998, a fire ravaged the mill and left it a shell of its former self. Prince William County has stepped in to help restore the building, and the hope is to make it open for visitors.

While the mill is interesting because of its connection with American history, it is also home to a rather gruesome ghost story. According to local lore, over one hundred years ago, a farmer and his family moved into the mill. His daughter gave her mother some spoiled meat, which she consumed. This caused the mother's death. Enraged by the loss of his wife, the farmer took a meat hook and hanged his daughter with it. Witnesses who have passed by the mill have claimed to see the daughter hanging inside the mill

Above: Beverly's Mill, circa 1930. The mill remained active until 1998. *Library of Congress.*

Opposite: The ruins of Beverly's Mill. *Author's collection.*

from a fourth-floor window. After the fire in 1998, the young girl's spirit had not been seen. Could the destruction of the mill have set her spirit free?

Another local ghostly legend occurred one hundred years ago. A man simply known as Mike liked to visit some of the taverns in the area of the Gap and to have a few drinks. One night, after enjoying his own spirits, he stumbled his way through the dark and fell down on the road, only to have his head severed off his body by a passing vehicle. Since that fateful night, people who have traveled through the Gap have claimed to come across poor headless Mike, who now carries his head in hopes of finding someone who may be able to affix it back on his body.

CLOVERLAND

Built in the 1790s, this home looked like it could have come out of a classic horror film. With that being said, it should come as a surprise to no one that the house was haunted.

Two ghosts were noted to have existed in the home. The first was that of a woman who was often described as very friendly and who was accompanied by the sounds of ruffling when she moved. The other spirit was that of a headless man who carried his head with him. While the second ghost could have been made up to scare children or could even be Mike of Thoroughfare Gap, the tale has more credibility attached to it than one would imagine. The man who first told the tale was John Hill Carter, the son of the builder of Cloverland. He claimed to have seen the spirit moving about the house and said he saw his father having a discussion with the spirit. What this discussion was about is anyone's guess.

Today, the remnants of Cloverland is a small cemetery plot where members of the Carter family were buried. The land where the house used to stand had fallen on hard times and almost became a landfill for the county. However, thanks to efforts from members of the historical community, along with land deed documents showing that the Carter family still owned the land where Cloverland stood, the last remnants of the property remain as a silent testament to its haunted past.

4

BRISTOW

One of the largest-growing communities in Prince William County is the area known as Bristow. Located on the Bristow Road, this community was built on the land owned by the Linton family known as Ford Plantation. During the Civil War, the Battle of Bristoe Station was fought near the family land. In this battle, Union forces were able to drive Confederate forces from Prince William County and effectively secure the county for the Union for the remainder of the war.

The Linton family owned the land until 1894, when Sarah Linton converted to Catholicism and became a Benedictine nun. With her conversion, Sarah Linton decided to donate her land to the Church with the understanding that the land would be used to create schools for impoverished boys and girls.

In 1922, a military school was created on the Linton family land. This school would remain a military academy until 1989. In that year, the school became coeducational, and the majority of the land used by the school was sold to developers. Today, the Linton Hall School is still run by the Benedictine nuns and is a landmark in the area.

BRENTSVILLE COURTHOUSE

Brentsville, Virginia, is located on the Bristow Road, which runs across the majority of the county. The small town founded early in the 1800s was seemingly the perfect location for the county seat due to its central location in the county, the prospect of building canals to connect the western half of the county to the east and the rapid decline of prominence for the town of Dumfries. The courthouse was built in 1822, adding another reason to make the town the new county seat for Prince William County. This structure would wear many hats over the years, including being a dormitory for a girls' school, a private home and an office space.

The small, rural town of Brentsville, however, would lose its status of being the county seat namely because of the remoteness of its location. Instead, the growing city of Manassas would take that honor, largely due to its prominence as a railroad junction. Today, the small, rural community is the kind of town where if you blink you could miss it. When driving along the main road, a driver need only count to thirty, and they'll discover that their car has covered the entire distance of the town.

What the town lacks in size, it makes up for in ghostly occurrences. Many people have talked about experiences in both the courthouse and jailhouse. The courthouse has been restored to the way it looked in 1830, and visitors who tour the historic structure have in mind the idea of ghosts lurking around the property. The experiences of these guests have tended to be identical in that they hear the sounds of knocking in the buildings and see the occasional apparitions.

The Brentsville Courthouse and Jailhouse. *Author's collection.*

Brentsville Jailhouse. *Author's collection.*

The numerous sightings of spirits at the courthouse even led to the arrival of the famed Trans-Atlantic Paranormal Society, also known as T.A.P.S., whose show *Ghost Hunters* on the Sci-Fi channel led to a heightened exposure for the small community. After spending the night at the courthouse and jail, the team revealed that they did hear knocking in the jailhouse. These knocks would occur after questions were asked. The team also had an electromagnetic signal come up. The signal proved to be of greater interest to the team because the jail did not have any electricity. However, the most tantalizing of all the discoveries the team made was the thermal image of a body outside of the jail.

Who was this body? The haunted history of the jail might provide an answer. In 1872, James Clark was to be put on trial for the abduction of Fannie Fawell. After abandoning Fannie in Washington, D.C., Clark was arrested and later shot in his cell by Fannie's brother, Lucien Fawell. In a trial that should have been able to prove the guilt of Lucien, the jury declared the man innocent, with a voracious roar of approval from the spectators in the courtroom. According to the staff at the historic site, part of the reason Lucien was acquitted came from the fact that he, the judge and much of the jury were former Confederate soldiers. While bias was certainly heavy in this trial, some people argue that James Clark might have just cause for sticking around to haunt the jail because justice was not served. Then again, the argument could be made that James

Left: The jail cell where James Clark was killed in the middle of the night. *Author's collection.*

Below: The trees and open ground is where the gallows were built when it was time to conduct an execution in Brentsville. *Author's collection.*

Clark had been served justice by having his spirit permanently haunt the cell where he died.

Another ghost that has been claimed to haunt Brentsville is that of Agness, an enslaved woman who was hanged with another enslaved woman, named Katy, in 1839 for the murder of their master. Overall, the courthouse was the site of thirteen hangings, twelve of whom were African American. Their crimes included murdering their masters and trying to set the jail on fire. The exact location of their executions has been lost to history, but the general location of where the gallows were built is marked near a wooded field directly behind the courthouse. It is the story of Agness and the other enslaved people who were hanged at Brentsville that garners the most interest from ghost hunters and enthusiasts, as they want to hear more about their grisly demise than anything else.

INDEPENDENT HILL

Located near the end of the Bristow Road, Independent Hill was a small community that once boasted the Greenwood Gold Mine and is now the current home of the Prince William County School Board Complex. While the community is spread out, there is one particular story that comes from this unincorporated town that is unique and has a long history attached to it.

On December 12, 1868, an incident was first reported about Prince William County, detailing the sighting of an unusual creature. First published on December 25, 1868, and later reprinted on January 20, 1869, the article described how the farm of Silas Brown was being visited by a peculiar creature. The creature was described as "an immense figure…with large horns and terrible claws…three times as large as a man in its front, and having a back converging from its neck and shoulders, horizontally to the distance of some six or eight feet, and supplied on each side with huge and tremendous arms. It is of a pale bluish color when first seen, but on being irritated by the near approach of any person, becomes a deadly white, and issues from its surface a small volume of smoke, accompanied with a sickening smell."

According to Silas Brown, this creature had come to his farm multiple times and had even tried to attack him once. A neighbor of Silas Brown's, Mr. Siger, came to the Brown farm with his wife and happened to witness the arrival of the creature as well. Understandably skeptical, Mr. Siger accompanied Silas Brown outside toward the barn, when a large rock was hurled at him. The stone was so hot that Mr. Siger could not pick it up. He looked in the direction that it came from and saw the creature for the first time. According to Mr. Siger, it was "about fifty yards away and the air became filled and inoculated with brimstone."

After telling his wife about the incident, Mrs. Siger fell into a great fright and needed to be transported home. The entire community of Independent Hill became scared that a ghost, demon, monster or even the devil had come to their community to terrorize them. While no other articles appeared about the creature, the woods of Prince William Forest are still deep and cover a great deal of the county. Could there still be a creature lurking in the forest?

5

NOKESVILLE

In the westernmost portion of Prince William County, there is a small town called Nokesville. In many ways, it could be the perfect image of small-town America. After driving through its Main Street and seeing the row of buildings on either side, you will exit either side of the town into country land. The farms and cluster of trees and forests remind anyone who visits this part of Virginia that only a few miles outside of the Capital Beltway there is an area just this side of heaven.

Founded in 1859, Nokesville was named after James Nokes, who had originally owned the land that became the town. During the Civil War, the area where the town was going to be built would be the center for both Union and Confederate encampments. In addition to this, John S. Mosby and his rangers would frequent the area, and Confederate forces fought a small battle with Union forces at Kettle Run.

Following the war, the town became more prominent because of its location between Bristow and Catlett's Station on the Orange and Alexandria Railway. Although it only had two storefronts early in its existence, the arrival of a religious group known as the German Baptist Brethren allowed churches to be built in the area and helped bring banks, distilleries, doctors and other small businesses as well.

The primary resource of the town, however, was agriculture. With farms surrounding the town in every direction, many businesses found in Nokesville dealt with farming equipment. By the latter half of the twentieth century, Nokesville was turning into a ghost town, as there were more businesses than people. With passenger trains no longer coming into Nokesville, many of the old structures still remain empty, with the occasional antique shop or restaurant popping up in the town. Despite this, the old farming community does provide a story about its past that helps to bring a chill to the spines of the children who live around Nokesville.

BROADLANDS FARM

Broadlands Farm, just outside of the town of Nokesville, is home to a spirit affectionately referred to as Ruth. While this may or may not be her name, her presence has been felt for many years. This is the story of a young woman who still haunts her home and wants anyone living there to understand that while they may be the physical occupants of the building today, she will forever be the resident of the home.

How she came to haunt the home is rather unclear, but previous occupants of the home claimed that the building was a field hospital during the Civil War. Ruth was working in the house and was shot. The earliest known incidents of Ruth making her presence known to the occupants of her former home came as the scent of lavender, but its source of origin could never be determined.

While scents are often associated with spirits, most people who are interested in ghosts want more tangible evidence. For them, it is necessary to introduce Connie Minnick. Her family owned Broadlands, and she found herself encountering Ruth in various ways. Her earliest recollection of the spirit came in the form of hearing a skirt rustling on the stairs. This particular incident can be chalked up to a child's imagination or misinterpreting movement inside of a house. Connie insisted, however, that Ruth would create some manifestations of herself, but she would make her presence felt in three specific ways.

The first came with a picture. The Minnick family came into possession of a framed portrait of Ulysses S. Grant. After looking through the house for a suitable location for it, they found the perfect spot to hang the picture. As soon as it went up, the picture came back down with an earth-shattering crash. After a few attempts at rehanging the picture and discovering it returned to the ground each time, the family decided to replace the picture with a mirror. Ironically, the mirror weighed twice the amount of the Grant picture, yet oddly, it never once budged from its wall.

General Ulysses S. Grant. *Library of Congress.*

The other two instances dealt with the same theme: fire. On two separate occasions, there was an opportunity for the house to be burned down, yet through some otherworldly force, it did not. The first occurred when a log rolled out of the fireplace without anyone realizing it. By the time someone did see the fiery log, they were amazed that the flames were confined only to the log and nowhere else. The second fiery event occurred when a fire broke out in the attic of the home. Since the building was old, and dried wood burns much faster than newer wood, the family was dumbfounded when the fire seemed to contain itself in the attic and refused to move into any other part of the house. Was Ruth protecting her home from potential damage? The Minnicks believed that was the case.

6

BULL RUN

Beginning in a little spring found in the Bull Run Mountains in Loudoun County and continuing east across Loudoun and into Prince William County, Bull Run Creek acts as a natural, physical boundary between Fairfax, Loudoun and Prince William Counties. The creek continues its flow east to the Occoquan River, which then flows into the Potomac River. From the moment the first settlers started to work their way west across the county to settle along waterways and create communities until July 20, 1861, Bull Run was simply a line on the map of Virginia that held very little significance.

On July 21, 1861, the First Battle of Bull Run (Union name) or Manassas (Confederate name) was fought along the creek. During the early portion of the battle, the Union army was able to drive the Confederate troops back but soon found themselves retreating toward the creek in a panic. As the men raced across the bridge, Confederate artillery shells began to fall around the bridge. While many would make it across and back to safety, some would not. Those who were not able to make their way to safety found themselves forever immortalized at the field where they fell.

THE BATTLEFIELD

"You can't prove anything by me," said James Burgess, a park ranger at Manassas Battlefield, in 1989. He had spent many years hearing stories about ghosts still residing on the field that saw the first great battle of the Civil War. The stories shared to the park rangers by guests included hearing the sounds of gunshots, smelling burning powder and even seeing spirits in the dusk hours on the battlefield. With so many different locations where people have seen spirits on the field, it is easy to confuse one story with another. However, there are a few specific locations on the field that seem to focus the energies of the ghosts.

The simple building near the visitor center known as Henry House is often visited by tourists on the Manassas battlefield. The original structure found itself in the middle of the bloodiest portion of the battle as Confederate artillery fought Union infantry for control of the hill that the house rested on. Union artillery, fearing Confederates were inside the house and using it for sharpshooters, pointed their cannons at the home and began to fire it. The resulting damage led to the building's destruction. It would not be until 1870 that the home would be reconstructed on top of the ruins of its predecessor.

While the outside story of the home fascinates many, the inside story of the home proves to be greater than anyone could possibly have imagined. Mrs. Judith Carter Henry lived in the Henry House when the first official battle of the Civil War began. Unable to leave, she decided to stay in her home and allow the battle to pass her by. Confederate soldiers, surprised by her presence and realizing her impending danger, quickly worked to move the immobile Mrs.

The reconstructed Henry House at the Manassas National Battlefield. *Author's collection.*

The tombstone of Judith Hill, who died as a result of her wounds during the First Battle of Manassas. *Author's collection.*

Henry from her home to safety. As they began to transport her, the continual fire of artillery prevented anyone inside the house from knowing a shell was coming right toward them until it finally shattered through the wall and into the bodies of those trying to escape the building. Mrs. Henry was severely wounded, and her foot was ripped from her body. She and the other wounded Confederates were evacuated from the building, but the combination of her wounds and age resulted in her death.

Since the reconstruction of the home and its donation to the National Park Service in 1940, visitors to the Henry House have reported, on numerous occasions, seeing a woman dressed in white standing in the family cemetery in front of the home. In one rare instance, a visitor quickly lifted his video camera to record the spirit in front of the graves to prove the existence of ghosts. Sadly, future viewers found the tape to be too shaky to make a conclusive decision on whether this spirit was that of Mrs. Henry or if it was something else altogether. Others commented that the film had to have been a fake and that the person captured on film was nothing more than a hoax.

Searching for this film on YouTube, this writer was given a unique opportunity to see a "ghost" on film and begin to make comments on it.

Soldier's Monument.
Library of Congress.

After viewing the footage, the critique is simply this: while the ghost of Mrs. Henry may be real, the video did not capture her. Instead, it captured a person who chose to wear white on a particularly warm day in Virginia and was walking by as the would-be filmmaker was taking his video.

Even though Mrs. Henry's spirit can be described as hard to pin down, another location close to her home has been reported to have the spirits of the dead nearby, and they often make appearances.

The Soldier's Monument, found directly behind the Henry House, has a plaque on it that reads, "In Memory of the Patriots Who Fell at Bull Run, July 21, 1861." As visitors walk up to the monument to pay their respects to those first few hundred men who died on both sides of the battle, some tourists discover that they are not always alone.

Both visitors and park rangers have described seeing soldiers standing at the base of the monument giving their own silent vigils. These soldiers appear at all times during the day, but their appearances tend to rise during the summertime. Does this mean these soldiers appear closer to when they died? Or that these men wish to remember the battles in which they were involved? The answers to those questions are subject to debate and are usually reserved to those who ask and consider the questions very carefully.

Whether or not a person believes in ghosts, the fact that the soldiers who were at the battle appear on a frequent basis is never in doubt. Many times, soldiers are seen standing by trees or walking along the battlefield. In one instance, a soldier was seen by a large walnut tree close to the Henry House farm site. When tourists went to speak with the soldier, he was gone. Reenactors and other historians who go to the battlefield tend to stay close to the visitor's center to answer questions and have a full view of the field. Park rangers have confirmed that these individuals do not like to trek out toward the Henry House and prefer to stay closer to the building and its air conditioning.

Another instance of people seeing a soldier on the field occurred close to the monument of the Fifth New York Zouave Regiment. During the Second Battle of Bull Run, this regiment acted as a human shield for the retreating Union army to allow it to get back to the protective ring of forts that surrounded Washington. After suffering massive casualties, the remnants of the regiment retreated and joined the rest of the army. Their sacrifice would be remembered with a monument built in the location where they made their gallant stand. Visitors to this monument have described numerous encounters with strange and haunting events. Many of the stories involved deal with sudden temperature drops on the field, even when it is an extremely hot day, or the sudden smell of gunpowder around the monument. In some cases, visitors have seen members of the forlorn regiment appear and disappear, usually around sunset.

The sightings of the Zouaves have occurred so many times that many ghost hunters have gone to see if they can capture images of the spirits on film. In one particular instance, a group of ghost hunters had witnesses with them who saw the Zouave ghosts, but when the film was developed, the pictures all came out blank.

Another story dealt with a former employee and his family who were on the field and encountered a ghost. The spirit seemed to have been beckoning the father to come and follow. According to the family, the features of the ghost were nondescript. The father of the family claimed it was an out-of-body experience and began to go toward the spirit. He did not know what would happen next but said that his daughter grabbed hold of his arm, screamed and brought him back to his body. As he put it, "We're God-fearing people; we don't know if it was the work of God or the Devil."

Of all the stories of people encountering spirits at the battlefield, one of the most chilling came when a park ranger was leading a tour near the Henry House

The New York Monument at the Manassas National Battlefield. *Author's collection.*

and heard the sound of a commotion behind him. Believing it was a child or a group of children making the noise, the ranger looked back but only saw a little wind twister pulling up some leaves and moving around. Realizing his error, the ranger went back to his tour, and the twister disappeared a few moments later. His group, however, would tell a different version of what they saw for the rest of the tour. According to witnesses, while the ranger was facing them, the group focused its attention not on the battlefield but on the ground behind him. As the ranger spoke, the grass showed footprints walking across the ground behind him.

Even though some groups of visitors see ghosts on the battlefield, there are a few strong-willed individuals who will go over every square inch of the field and visit every site that held importance to history. Off in the woods leading toward Centreville is the Stone Bridge. This bridge proved to be of great tactical importance during the First Battle of Bull Run. As Confederate forces under the command of General Thomas Jonathan Jackson chased the fleeing Union army, the retreating Northern soldiers made a beeline toward the bridge and the safety of the northern end of Bull Run. Sadly, their mad dash found them charging straight for a traffic jam that could rival any found today.

Northern civilians, fancying an opportunity to witness a battle, became frightened and concerned for their own safety as the Confederates began to push the Union army back. Jumping into their buggies and wagons, the civilians made their own mad dash for the Stone Bridge. The temporary log jam created panic among the early arrivers. After surviving the ordeal, it was no small wonder that the Union army made it through the battle and was able to eventually fight another day.

Even though the retreat was disastrous, the memory of it for those who were there left an imprint of their memories on the ground where they stood on that frightening day. Adventurous visitors to the battlefield who come out to the bridge say they can hear the sounds of soldiers marching across the bridge and going across the creek below it. Others have said that while they are there at night, they can see the muzzle flashes of cannons being fired through the trees. One ghost hunter, Beth Brown, was recording audio clips in hopes of hearing soldiers marching by the bridge. She noted a bit of movement from her peripheral vision, but when she turned to look, there was nothing there. For her, it was the closest thing to a ghost on that particular expedition to the field.

Farther away from the popular parts of the Manassas Battlefield is the Stone House, which was used as a field hospital for both Northern and Southern armies. Numerous soldiers died in the building, and their spirits have been known to haunt the structure. Many people have claimed to hear the sounds of gunshots being fired. During the early 1900s, the Stone House was referred to by some living in Manassas as the haunted house.

This particular reputation would continue to be more bizarre and frightening as the years went by, with numerous stories coming out about ghosts being in the house. In one instance, two park rangers were closing up the building when they heard the sound of footsteps on the floor above them. Thinking that they had somehow missed a tourist in their final sweep of the house, the two men went upstairs to look. When they arrived, they found no one in the building. The front door was locked, and there was no way for anyone trying to stay in the building after hours to hide from the park rangers. There were no closets in the house, and it was empty of furniture at the time. The two rangers, with their nervousness beginning to show, decided to do the only thing that any of us would do in a situation like this—run away.

Another park ranger found himself dealing with a spirit at the Stone House in a rather peculiar situation. The ranger was a seasonal employee. During certain parts of the year, there can be stretches of time when there will not be any visitors to the building. It was during this time that the ranger found that the quietness and loneliness of the Stone House afforded him a few moments to close his eyes. Like any of us who have found ourselves in this position, the ranger soon began to go from a momentary closing of the eyes into a full-blown nap. As he began to doze off, he was suddenly awoken when his glasses were slapped off of his face and went flying across the room. The ranger retrieved his glasses and searched the house, trying to find the culprit responsible for interrupting his nap. But he was alone in the house. Could it have been a spiritual officer or an unhappy ghost of a sergeant seeing the ranger asleep and deciding to give him a rough wake-up call?

The Stone Bridge is where it is said that the sounds of ghosts marching can be heard. *Author's collection.*

Many wounded soldiers died in makeshift hospitals like the Stone House on Manassas National Battlefield. *Library of Congress.*

While this story sounds chilling and frightening, there is another tale that tries to one-up, with a ghost following a person home on a family vacation. A visitor to the house claimed to have seen a spirit while looking inside the house. Stunned by the sight of the ghost, he returned to his family, only to discover that the spirit decided to come with him. The ghost continually appeared to the young man for the rest of his family vacation. When this young man's trip was complete and he returned home, the ghost no longer appeared to him. Thinking the most frightening aspect of the trip was over, the young man developed his photos, only to get one last scare. In a picture he took of his family standing in front of the Stone House, there knelt the soldier he saw right at the corner of the house staring directly at him and the camera.

While ghosts may like to follow people home, what happens when they decide to trick you into seeing things or possibly not seeing things? This particular phenomenon occurred to a Northern Virginia resident by the name of Kathleen Luisa. In 1986, Ms. Luisa was driving along Route 29 with her family heading toward the battlefield to see Halley's Comet. Ms. Luisa was looking for Sudley Road, which intersects Route 29. The physical landmark for this intersection is the Stone House. If you're driving north, the house is on the left. If you're driving south, the house is on the right. As Luisa and her family drove southbound looking for the house, they could not find their intersection and thought they drove right through it.

It dawned on Luisa that she had gone too far when she started seeing signs for Gainesville. Turning around, the family returned to where Route 29 and Sudley Road intersected and looked toward where the Stone House was supposed to be. Instead of seeing the house, they stared directly into an empty lot. The entire family swore that the house appeared to have been moved completely. Disheartened by the loss of a historical building, the family returned home. Two weeks later, Ms. Luisa was driving south on Route 29 and discovered the Stone House was back. It was as if the house had never disappeared. While skeptics could argue that the family's eyes might have been playing tricks on them, to this day, Kathleen Luisa and her family stand firm by their claims that the house actually disappeared.

For those who have heard this story, the concept of a house, much less a stone one, disappearing sounds too fanciful to be true. However, the story was corroborated in 1997 by Beverly Kish. Having lived in Northern Virginia for twenty years, she was familiar with many of the landmarks in the area and knew exactly where the Stone House was. The biggest difference between her tale and that of the previous one is that on the night she saw the Stone House disappear, there was a full moon. With the light of the moon, Kish knew she had arrived at the correct intersection, only to discover that the house was gone. Her initial belief was that the house was moved, but after learning about the 1986 incident, she knew she had just been a witness to a ghostly occurrence.

Of all the stories, the most conclusive one that proves the existence of ghosts in the Stone House is the story of Jane Becker. The Stone House had some period furniture put in, and Ms. Becker went inside to take a few photographs with her 35mm camera. When the pictures were developed, she was pleased with each shot except for one. The one picture in question had a strange white blotch in the middle of it, but it also became transparent. She could see the security rope that blocked visitors from the furniture through the transparent potion of the blotch.

Checking the lens for any sign of a smudge or something that could have created the blotch, she decided to get professional assistance in determining how the blotch appeared on her picture. She had the photograph and its negative sent to Kodak, the manufacturer of the film, to be tested. When the results came in, she had the picture and its negative take a small trip to the Federal Bureau of Investigation for analysis. Both groups came back with the same result: there was nothing wrong with the picture or the negative. The blotch was not added into the picture, nor could it possibly have been faked. In this one instance, Jane Becker captured what she has since come to affectionately refer to as the Stone House Ghost.

Ben Lomond

The Ben Lomond Plantation was used by Confederate forces during the First Battle of Manassas as a field hospital. Hospitals have been known to be a center of ghostly activities that result in many ghost stories. In one circumstance, a Prince William County employee spent the night at Ben Lomond during a weekend of Halloween programs. While sleeping there, the employee felt "a sudden sensation of being dragged." When the employee awoke, he found himself dragged across the room. Was he confused for a dead body by a ghost?

While being confused for a dead body might frighten some people, there could be some merit in the story, as another account from a ghost hunter also reported feeling a tug on his jacket that came out of nowhere. His daughter

Ben Lomond, where the spirits of Confederate soldiers still remain. *Author's collection.*

was with him during this particular event and said that she had never seen her father so scared in her life. To further confirm their suspicions about the presences of ghosts in the building, there was an audio recording of a ghost admitting to tugging on the jacket and a second ghost claiming her name was Kat. These events certainly helped the pair know that there was a ghostly presence in the building.

According to employees of the Prince William County Historic Preservation Department, audio recordings were done in the house by other ghost hunters. When they did this, the hunters were able to capture a voice clearly saying "Georgia." While some members of the department felt this was inaccurate, further research revealed that there were soldiers from a Georgia regiment who died outside of the house in the garden. Was the voice heard on the tape one of the soldiers?

So, what causes these spirits to remain? Since the building was used as a hospital, many amputations occurred to soldiers on both their arms and legs, which caused many men to die premature deaths. A large amount of blood was lost in the building, and a great deal of it was soaked into the floorboards. When going to the basement of the building, firefighters from the county have been able to verify that some of the floorboards are still soaked with the blood of the patients who were operated on directly from above. Could this persistent blood be what helps create an anchor for the ghosts to remain in the building?

7

MANASSAS

As the railroad industry began to spread throughout Northern Virginia, a tiny crossroad was created in Prince William County and named Manassas Junction. During the Civil War, the small rail station would become famous with two separate battles fought in the vicinity. In the First Battle of Manassas, the junction proved to be critical for Confederate forces, as reinforcements from the Shenandoah Valley helped to turn the tide of the battle from a possible Union victory to a complete Confederate victory.

Following the battle, the junction was briefly used by the Confederates as a supply depot but was abandoned and later used by the Union for the same purpose until 1862. After the Second Battle of Manassas, the Union still controlled the area but opted to no longer use the railroad junction for military purposes. The Confederates had been able to plunder the supplies of the Union army and exposed the dangers of using the junction for a major military supply depot.

Shortly after the war, Manassas grew to be an incorporated town. With this rise in prominence, leaders in the town attempted to campaign for a transfer of the county seat away from Brentsville. Many promises were made, but it was not until 1892 that Manassas succeeded in becoming the seat of the county government. With the transfer of power officially made from the eastern half of the county to the western, Manassas was the center of authority in Prince William County. The reason for Manassas's ability to remain the center of government was threefold: it had the benefit of being named the county seat, it had a railroad junction and it was seen as a gateway to country living by means of the railroad. Manassas would become an independent city in the boundaries of Prince William County in 1975.

While the battlefield outside of the town provided a great deal of tourism for Manassas, people interested in looking for ghosts would soon discover that there was more to Manassas than simply a battlefield. The town itself painted a unique portrait of ghostly events that added more character to the region.

OLDE TOWNE INN

The next time you visit a hotel, it might be a good idea to double-check on whether the place you plan on spending the night is haunted. The present building of the Olde Towne Inn is only about fifty years old, but according to those who remember, the site has been used as a hotel for more years than the current building. Despite the varying accounts of the age of parts of the building, one aspect that remains a constant is the ghosts who reside in the hotel.

According to most people, the three most haunted rooms in the hotel are rooms 50, 52 and 54. One couple reported that when they stayed in room 54, they heard the sound of crashing items as they slept. On investigating the noise, the two found nothing amiss. A little later in the night, they felt a tugging on their mattress. Fearing a rodent in the room, they turned on the lights and checked to see if there was anything there. Thinking their imaginations were getting the better of them, the couple went back to sleep. While the first two events were easy to try to forget, the third event was much harder to ignore. Waking up in the night, the wife discovered that her husband was levitating over the floor and suddenly dropped straight to it.

One room over is a ghost known as Miss Lucy. She spends most of her time haunting room 52, which is located in the older portion of the hotel. For the most part, her haunting could be described as prank-like and childish. She creates scratching sounds, messes up beds in rooms that were already cleaned, unplugs appliances and occasionally manifests herself in a form that can be seen by everyone.

However, one day, for reasons unknown, Miss Lucy decided to go further than she had ever gone before. In 1991, a different couple was spending the night at the Olde Towne Inn and was sleeping in bed when they were awakened by the feeling of a heavy presence in the bed with them. An hour later, the man felt himself being elevated from the bed and then being unceremoniously thrown down to the floor.

The road sign for the Olde Towne Inn in Manassas, Virginia. *Author's collection.*

Has Miss Lucy decided to leave room 52 and also haunt room 54? It seems likely, as the majority of the stories that emerge from rooms 50, 52 and 54 involve people being pulled from beds. However, there does appear to be another spirit in the hotel.

Two men who enjoyed ghost hunting were spending the night in room 34 and were hoping to have a supernatural experience. With their equipment set up, they started to take readings of the room and found that barometric changes were occurring in the room at various points of time. Temperature changes, namely changes where the air feels colder, are one of the first signs of spirits being present in a room.

One of the two men claimed to be extremely sensitive to spirits and claimed to sense at least eight presences around him. Some people could argue that they can feel any number of presences around them if the mood is set right. To be fair, if your mindset is that something is going to happen, then your imagination will go ahead and allow it to happen. At the same time though, who is to say that this person was not accurate in his assessment?

As the two men prepared for bed, they both hoped to have an experience. It is at this point that both men claimed that the night took on some rather strange twists and turns. Both men claimed to feel the room get warmer and a shaking going on inside of them, like a train passing through their bodies. One awoke and attempted to move but felt as if something was pushing him down and keeping him from getting up.

Though they have not seen any ghosts, there have been numerous occurrences of people being physically stopped by ghosts for unknown reasons. Were these men two more people the ghosts were trying to keep down? Were they unwilling participants in a reenactment of a spirit's physical demise? Perhaps we will never know.

THE THINGS I LOVE

Just a few feet away from the old post office building, there once was a shop called The Things I Love. Joanne Wunderly, former owner of the business, said the building was haunted but not by vengeful spirits. Instead, she believed the ghosts in question were those of Sallie and Nellie Hazen, two women who had, at one time, operated a hat store at the same location.

The store was the oldest existing storefront in all of Old Town Manassas, due to a large fire that destroyed much of the downtown in 1905. When Joanne set up her office on the second floor of the building, she found that every room had a penny in it. It seemed strange to her, but she also took it as a sign of good luck. She also discovered something odd about her office: "The door would shut…just shut."

The strangest but also most fortuitous event that occurred happened to Joanne in 1997. She had created a fall display that used a lit candle. Every day before she left, Joanne would blow out the candle. One day, she returned to the store after picking up a friend's daughter from ballet class and discovered the candle was lit and about to set the store on fire. Joanne quickly put the fire out and saved her business. Had the Hazen sisters made her want to go back and check the store? No one can say for certain, but Joanne does admit that she went back to the store for nothing very important but was glad she did.

OLD TOWN HALL

In 1914, Manassas built a new town hall after much of the downtown was destroyed by fire. Like many buildings in the early twentieth century, this structure was used for multiple purposes. In this particular case, the structure was used as both a police and fire station. In the 1950s, the building became exclusively the town hall, until 1986, when the current town hall was

The Old Town Hall was used for many different purposes, including a jail. *Author's collection.*

completed. As different city employees began working in the building, many started to report that a door in the building would open and close on its own. When employees found their way into the room with the mysterious opening and closing door, they discovered an extra surprise was in store for them, as the door, once shut, was locked.

Many city employees believe the ghost is a friendly one, but according to Jim Robinson, a former firefighter and longtime resident of Manassas, the ghost had an interesting past. As Robinson explained, the ghost may have been a prisoner who was arrested in the 1930s who hanged himself with his belt in his jail cell because he felt ashamed of getting arrested for the crime he committed. While Robinson was willing to give a possible clue to the identity of the ghost, he was not willing to say that the cause of the door opening and closing was a ghost.

Robinson stated that he believed the reason the door opened and closed at random was due to a draft in the building. This particular theory was seconded by the former director of the Manassas Museum, Scott Harris. Harris believed the door lacked the necessary tension to hold the door shut and would easily bounce off of the door frame before a person realized what happened. While skeptics might look for rational explanations for events attributed to ghosts, Harris was willing to concede that it was "more interesting to consider a spirit doing it."

8

DEATH AND SOCIETY

RELIGION AND DEATH

When we think of death, most people begin to think about the religious implications of it and ensuring that the deceased receives a proper send-off into the afterlife. Is there an afterlife? Does the deceased even know what is going on? While the former question is a little more difficult to answer, the latter proves that the deceased is deeply concerned about making sure that their grand exit from the world stage is anything but forgettable and inappropriate.

As an example, there are a few hallmarks worth noting of how a body is prepared for death in the Roman Catholic faith. First, the body must be laid out neatly to be viewed. No one wants to look at a body that appears to have been thrown into the coffin. Families always have the option to have the lid open or closed before and during a funeral, but even if the coffin lid is closed, it is best to have the body laid out properly.

Second, lighting is essential for the body. Strange as it may seem, both funerals and wakes are never dark affairs. Instead, the body is always well lit when it comes to funerals. In many ways, this stems from our belief that the spirit must be led to a better place, as the world of the living is now dark while the afterlife is filled with light. Another aspect of light being associated with death is that the light represents the life of the deceased, but once the light is blown out or extinguished, the person is no longer alive. This particular aspect is more morbid in modern society, as we always try to find ways to ensure that while the physical life may be gone, the spiritual life remains strong and alive.

Third, a crucifix is given to the deceased. The form of the crucifix has varied from generation to generation. Some people have a full cross in one hand while others will hold a rosary. Fourth, holy water is sprinkled onto the body to help consecrate it. In the Catholic faith, a child enters the faith by being purified with holy water. As they leave the mortal faith, bodies are given one last purification to help make them worthy of entering heaven.

Finally, the body is buried in a consecrated place. The majority of people are buried in cemeteries, though there are rare exceptions when the person does not find their body going into the ground. In the cases of sea burials, the consecration of the body and purification of the body through holy water allows it to be buried at sea, since the process of preparing the body for burial makes that particular location consecrated ground.

Another tradition that has evolved when it comes to Christian burial is that the body used to have to face toward the east when buried. The belief was that when the resurrection of Christ occurred, it would happen in the east, and this would allow the deceased to be raised from the dead and look directly into the second coming.

While the Christian faith in all of its denominations is still the largest religious group in Prince William County, both Islam and Judaism have customs regarding death that mirror the Christian traditions while offering unique differences. In the case of Judaism, funerals occur as soon as possible after death. In some cases, funerals will occur as soon as twenty-four hours and up to forty-eight hours after death. It is only in rare circumstances that the funeral will be much later than this time period to allow distant relatives to arrive.

The deceased will have a ritual washing, known as a *tahara*, and the body is then dressed in a plain burial shroud. During the funeral, the rabbi will begin with the cutting of a black ribbon, which symbolizes the breaking away from loved ones. Following the funeral, the family will enter into a seven-day mourning period known as *shiva*. This time will see members of the family break from their normal routines as a symbol of the disruption that death has caused for them. It also shows grief through self-sacrifice.

While Christians and Jews see death as an end, Muslims do not. Instead, they view death as a transition from one state of being to another. Depending on how a person has lived their lives, the deceased will either be rewarded with the separation of the world's ugliness from their souls or punished with the removal of all the world's beauty.

GENDER, FASHION AND TRADITIONS

We look at death as a passing of one life into the next and wish to fondly remember the one we lost in the best possible light. In the past, the same thing could be said, but there were some differences.

In announcing the death of an individual, the local church bells would begin to ring to announce to the community that a person had passed away. For a woman, the bell would ring six times, while men would have the bell rung eight times. Following the gender tolls, the bell would ring once for each year of the person's life. These bells, often referred to as passing bells, were also used by some people as a method of scaring away evil spirits from the body.

Following the funeral, a procession would lead the body to the cemetery. Men and woman had only two events in their lives in which they were the center of attention: marriage and burial. The procession would be led by a preacher. If the person who died was a man, then the men would follow the preacher. Alternately, if the person was a woman, then it would be the women who followed.

Even the method of mourning between the genders has often been scrutinized. It has always been seen that women are permitted to cry at funerals and be vocal in their wailing. Men, meanwhile, are not expected to show their grief in public but must instead hide their remorse behind masks of unperturbed silence and a grim understanding that a person they once knew is gone.

Black has often been the color worn to indicate that a person is in mourning for the loss of a loved one. The color was chosen because black matched the color of night and darkness. In addition, it was deemed the best color to describe a soul abandoned to grief and the most respectful to wear. But black was not always the color to be worn. In fact, the original mourning color was white. Royalty changed that tradition, and the lower classes soon followed suit. While there have been those who have thumbed their noses at convention and worn whatever they wanted to a funeral or during a period of mourning, black has withstood the test of time for almost six hundred years.

One tradition that has not been well practiced today but meant a great deal in the past is how a person was buried in the ground. Today, we place bodies with their backs lowered into the ground. This tradition has had a resounding effect on all of us, as sometimes we think about the deceased and say that the person might be rolling over in their grave because of something

Pallbearers bearing a coffin into church from caisson. A funeral procession would escort the body from the church to the cemetery. *Library of Congress.*

that had happened. Why do we say this? The answer is because at one time the dead were actually buried on their stomachs. The reason for this varied based on the culture, but there was one facet of being buried facedown that had a great deal of significance. If the body of the deceased was buried facing down, then someone wanted the family of the deceased to have ill will sent their way. An example of this would be the burying of a first-born facedown. Superstition states that if this were to occur, then there would be no new members of the family born.

A tradition that has greatly changed over the years is the cross markers on the side of roads. At one time, if a person died in an accident, the body of the deceased would be placed in the ground at the spot where they died, and a marker would then be placed over that spot. This particular tradition remained rather prominent in society through the 1700s. The most famous example of this was the burial of Major General Edward Braddock. During his ill-fated campaign to modern-day Pittsburgh, Braddock was mortally wounded and died while his men were retreating. George Washington had to stop British soldiers from burying Braddock on the side of the road where he died and instead had him buried in the road to prevent the body from being desecrated by Indians.

Left: Major General Edward Braddock was buried in the road where he died to protect his body from being desecrated. *Library of Congress.*

Right: Markers to indicate where people have died can still be found along many roads throughout Prince William County and Northern Virginia. *Author's collection.*

Today, a memorial marker is on top of the body of General Braddock and next to the remnants of the original road on which Braddock marched. His body was discovered in the early 1800s and was moved to its current location. As for the tradition of burying a person at the spot of the accident, it has since fallen to the wayside, but the concept of keeping memorials to remember their deaths has continued to this date.

WAKING THE DEAD

Not to be confused with the hit AMC show *The Walking Dead* or the PBS show *Waking the Dead*, this particular term was taken more on a figurative level than literal. Waking the dead meant that a loved one or a couple who knew the deceased would remain with the body before the funeral. The reasons for this vary.

For those in the Jewish faith, the body was placed in a sepulcher, and family members would visit to mourn for the deceased. Prior to the funeral, though, a rabbi would remain with the body to make sure the deceased was dead. For Christians, the task of looking over a deceased individual allowed friends and family members to pray for that person's soul to help them get into heaven. It also allowed grieving family members to have people comfort them in their time of need. There are also the practical purposes involved. With this particular situation, the person who had to sit with the body was responsible for keeping the rats and other vermin from coming up to the deceased and beginning to eat them.

Waking the dead took on a slightly more literal meaning. During the eighteenth and nineteenth centuries, slipping into a coma or having an epileptic seizure was seen as a person being possessed or having a fit. While these episodes were common, the results often left onlookers under the impression that the poor individual who suffered from the condition had died. As a result, a coffin was quickly produced, a funeral was conducted and a burial took place. If the "deceased" happened to wake up during the first two stages, then they were truly lucky. In the event that the "deceased" woke up after the third stage, that poor individual found themselves buried alive.

This particular concern was so great that many individuals looked to ensure that they would not find themselves being buried alive. George Washington left explicit instructions that his body would be laid out in the New Room for three days before being buried in the family vault at Mount Vernon. Other people would ask that their bodies be laid out for friends and neighbors to say their final farewells but also to ensure that if they had not died, they had an opportunity to prevent an accidental burial.

To help prevent accidental burials from occurring too often, doctors began to tie strings connected to bells on the fingers of the corpses. If the person woke up and began to pull on the string, onlookers knew to rush to the coffin and save the person. Even in burial, the string was extended, and the bell was left on top of the grave just in case the person buried suddenly woke. In either situation, if the person were to ring the bell, it was said they were a dead ringer or they had been saved by the bell.

Picturing the Dead

It was originally referred to as *memento mori*. The concept was a simple one: a person should have some kind of physical remembrance of the deceased. Usually, the item in question might be a lock of hair that would be added to jewelry to be worn during the time of mourning and even some time after that. Today, we often take an item of a person for whom we had a great deal of love or respect. While all of this may seem normal, there is one aspect of the memento mori that takes remembering the dead to a whole new level.

As peculiar as it may seem, for some people, the concept of photographing the dead is a common habit. In many cases, the reason for this is due to family tradition and a need to remember their loved ones even up to the moment when they will no longer see them physically. This particular practice began in the mid-nineteenth century and was popular with families who had a baby who suddenly died. It was seen as part of the mourning process. For most members of the family, it was a memorial for the child. For the remaining members of the family, it was a way to remember their lost loved one, especially for the mother.

The trend continued to move away from photographing infants to include older children and adults. While the logic behind honoring and remembering the family members was still there, photographers proved that they had their own ideas as to how they should have the dead look. What follows may sound strange, but this may be where the inspiration for *Weekend at Bernie's* came into existence.

Unidentified deceased child. Families took pictures of lost children to remember them after death. *Library of Congress.*

People would either have the photographer come to them or bring the body to a photography studio. Once there, the body would be positioned in various poses to look life-like. This was taken to such extremes that different pieces of apparatuses were used to position the body into a standing position. Family members would also pose with the body to create a better illusion that the corpse was still living.

The thought of this can send shivers up and down the spine. However, when people learn that this practice is still done today, there is often a pause in the conversation where the listener has to take a moment to comprehend what they just heard.

CONTAINING THE DEAD

When it comes time to bury the dead, bodies of the deceased have had a long and hard road not only in Prince William County but also in the nation as a whole. When films show a person passing away and being buried long ago, there always seems to be a coffin being hastily made and the body placed into it. Contrary to popular belief, this particular practice is just a fiction created by our own understanding of death. Early settlers in the county who passed away would be buried in the ground either with or without something surrounding the body to protect it from the dirt being placed on top of it.

By the 1700s, people were beginning to change their attitude toward the dead and how they ought to be interred. Carpenters and cabinetmakers were being hired to measure a body and place it into a container to help preserve the body after death. In the following century, the practice of creating coffins became a full-time industry. It was also during the nineteenth century that a schism occurred over the method of burying a person.

Coffins have always been the mainstream term used to describe a vessel that a body is placed in for burial. A coffin is a wedge-shaped box that is wider toward the shoulders and becomes narrow toward the feet. Coffins were always simple and easy to work with for carpenters, and almost anyone could afford them. The wealthy, however, opted for something a little different. With a desire to show their wealth even in death, the term casket was expanded.

The original definition of *casket* was a jewel box. Due to its rectangular shape, caskets could be made larger and more ornate. The Hiller family

Some people take pictures of their deceased relatives at their funerals to have one last memory of their loved ones. *Library of Congress.*

of Massachusetts spent over seven years having their caskets built to their specifications. The builders received $40 a week for their work, finally totaling over $15,000. Mrs. Hiller even went so far as to demonstrate to friends how she would look inside her own casket.

Tombstones and Their Meanings

Why do tombstones exist? They do not look alike and often represent the different social classes and wealth associated with the families of the deceased, considering the cost that is associated with each stone. Still, the question persists. There are three primary principles for why tombstones exist. The first stems from the belief that the body dwells or sleeps in the grave, and people need to know who is there. The second reason follows from the first because future generations should know who this person was and what they did. The final reason is because the stone gives those who visit the grave a spot to pray over to help give religious comfort to the deceased.

When walking through cemeteries today, we see how the second reason for a tombstone has been used with success by different people who place different epitaphs and other decorations on their stones to remind those who are living about the personality of the deceased. Musical instruments, designs of a career and even pictures of the person when they were alive have been carved into tombstones. There are a handful of symbols that have a significant meaning when carved into the stone.

The most common symbols seen on tombstones are crosses, angels, clasped hands, praying hands and lambs. While these are often associated with Christianity, the reality is that each one of these symbols has more to it than meets the eye. For instance, a cross is not always a cross when it comes to the dead. It can symbolize a person's religion, such as a grave marked with a Greek or Latin cross. If a Celtic cross is placed on a grave, it is meant to let family members know the spirit is immortal and that death can never conquer it. If a Maltese cross is placed over the grave, it symbolizes the bravery of the deceased and can help strengthen that person's memory for those who are still living.

Clasped hands have been used to symbolize farewell and friendship. Meanwhile, praying hands have symbolized piety. Angels allow people to remember that there is an afterlife in heaven. Of all these symbols, the one that a majority of people recognize and can immediately place is perhaps the most peaceful of them all. The lamb is often thought of as a reference to Jesus being the lamb of God. However, another reference for the lamb can be found in youth. Many parents feel that they are shepherds when dealing with multiple children and will come up with many nicknames for their children, usually in the form of infant animals. A lamb is popular because of its innocence and general cuteness. As a result, the most common symbol placed on children's stones is that of a lamb.

While the lamb is commonly used for children, there are other symbols that are commonly seen and used to represent different people buried in the ground. An easy example is the Star of David for anyone who is Jewish. Another symbol is the crown, which signifies a noble or royal person. Anchors are often associated with sailors, while hearts are associated with love.

One symbol that is often mistaken is the skull and crossbones. The iconic image is usually associated with pirates, and many tour guides who take tourists through cemeteries will point to those particular graves and indicate that. If the guide told the truth, though, the symbol has more to it than meets the eye. Contrary to popular belief, the symbol does not represent the grave of a pirate. Instead, the symbol represents the finality of death. If this symbol can be easily misidentified, what about other symbols?

Tree trunks could represent a person who was a lumberjack, but that would be a mistake. If you look closer at the symbol and notice broken branches with the tree trunks, this indicates that the person's life was cut short. A scythe is another symbol used to describe this and is not the symbol of a farmer. An hourglass is used to describe the inevitability of death—not a timekeeper or watchmaker.

THE LADY OF DEATH

We think about death. We obsess about it. Sometimes, we realize it is inevitable and decide to fear it. Most times, we acknowledge death's inevitability and opt to live our lives to the fullest. In some rare cases though, some people decide to take death and try to explain how it has influenced our lives through the years. In Dale City, there is one woman who has done such a thing.

Her name is Georgia Meadows, and she has been referred to by her friends as the Lady of Death. This moniker was not given out of malice but rather due to her hobby of collecting items that relate to death and mourning. Georgia's home is full of nineteenth-century mourning art, clothes, pictures, jewelry and even a horse-drawn hearse from 1888. Her collection has led to issues with contractors who work on her home, as many find themselves uncomfortable working in rooms filled with coffins.

Although people might feel uncomfortable with the idea of a house filled with images and memorabilia of death, Georgia has gone one step further with her hobby by giving lectures on the topic. However, sometimes she gets a little more than she bargains for. While setting up for a lecture at the Manassas Museum, Georgia left a number of her mourning dresses set up on six mannequins. Reassured of the safety of the museum by security, Georgia went home knowing her mannequins were lined up in a row for easy viewing. The next morning, she returned to the museum and discovered the mannequins had been moved to stand next to each other and face each other. Georgia's response to this incident was to laugh and inquire if the ladies were having a good conversation.

Georgia's interest with ghosts began with the passing of her mother who, according to Georgia, started to haunt her home. As objects began to move throughout her kitchen, Georgia came to a reckoning with her mother's spirit, and she demanded that her mother stop trying to scare her. She told her to let her know she was at the home by shaking a plant. Sure enough, the plant started to shake.

The creepiest moment for Georgia and her hobby of collecting mementos of death came from a mourning dress made in the 1870s. After purchasing the dress at an antiques shop, Georgia placed it on a mannequin. While sitting at her sewing machine, Georgia noticed the dress begin to move and turn toward her. On seeing this, Georgia ran from the room. When she was able to summon enough courage, she returned to the room, took the dress off the mannequin and put it in a box. Perhaps it is possible to have too much of a certain thing.

9

GHOSTS OF A DIFFERENT KIND

On November 5, 2008, Governor Tim Kaine addressed the state of Virginia on the news that Barack Obama had been elected president of the United States. During his address, Kaine remarked, "Old Virginny is dead. We are a new and dynamic commonwealth....We are not living in the past. We are looking ahead." His words were profound. Virginia, which had voted Republican for decades, had just voted Democrat. The changing population of the state allowed for this change to occur, as more minorities began to enter Virginia and make their voices heard.

The *New York Times* once described Prince William County as "one of the mostly white, somewhat rural, far flung suburbs where Republican candidates went to accumulate votes to win elections in Virginia." Ironically, visitors to the county today will discover the name Prince William might be the whitest part of the county, as it has transformed into a multicultural community that might be seen as a window into the future of the nation—a majority minority population with a quiet but strong religious foundation that coexists in its boundaries.

For people like Bobby Ross Jr., religion is an extremely important part of the county's history and modern makeup. With almost half a million people in the county, churches can be found almost everywhere. To ignore the religious aspect of Prince William County, according to Bobby Ross Jr., makes it the ghost of the county. However, this may not be completely the case. Instead of calling religion *the* ghost of the county, perhaps referring to it as *a* ghost is more accurate. Religious views and politics do not necessarily mix today, but if it was possible to consider religion as a ghost, then what other ghosts could be found in Prince William County?

The easiest kind of ghost to consider and find is that of a perceived ghost. This type of spirit is one where we believe a place might be haunted but where there is no evidence to prove such a thing. Consider the following example: when driving along Hoadly Road in the middle of Prince William County, a driver comes to the end of the road with a decision to turn either left or right onto Route 234. If the driver turns left, the corner of his or her eye might come across an old abandoned farmhouse on the side of the road. This structure is easy to miss, as it is beginning to get lost behind unkempt trees and bushes. While the structure could take on the role of a home for a family, it also has the ability to give off an eerie feeling that there could be otherworldly dwellers inside its walls.

Another structure with this kind of reputation is the caretaker's home at Rippon Lodge. While areas around the home have had their own tragic and haunted histories, the building does not appear to have any ghosts in it despite its rather ominous basement stone walls and heavy barred windows. Some staff believe the basement could be or even should be haunted, but after speaking with managers and historians at the site, there has never been any evidence or stories of a haunting occurring in the basement. Instead, the basement might have been the location of a warehouse at one time in the eighteenth and nineteenth centuries. If this was the case, then the only ghost there might be that of past business dealings.

Even though our imaginations can get carried away, our capacity to think about the past does allow us to look at places and ponder about what once was. As a result, the ghosts of past people come to the forefront of our minds. One such ghost of past people is that of the Native Americans. U.S. Highway 1, or Route 1, was once referred to by Native Americans as the Potomac Path. Interestingly, the word *Potomac* means "trader" in the language of the Doeg Indians. Other Doeg terms that are still in use in Prince William County are in plain sight. *Quantico*, where the marine base is located, means "by the long stream." Meanwhile, *Marumsco* means "at the island rock."

With words from the past ingrained in the local landscape, the spirit of those who used to live in Prince William County remains alive and well in a different form. There is a sign on the side of Route 234 (Dumfries Road) that indicates where campers can go to enter the camping ground of the Prince William National Forest. This scenic national park is one that countless people visit to get in touch with nature. Yet this entrance is the

Left: This abandoned home near the intersection of Dumfries Road and Hoadly Road looks haunted, but are there really ghosts inside? *Author's collection.*

Below: The basement façade of the caretaker's house at Rippon Lodge looks like it could be haunted, but staff members are quite confident it is not. *Author's collection.*

Left: A rock formation in Prince William Forest that looked like a makeshift grave. *Author's collection.*

Right: The tombstone of Robert Taylor, located inside the Prince William County Forest. *Author's collection.*

ghost of a different past. The campground entrance was, at one time, the entrance for African Americans who wanted to camp in the forest during the days of segregation.

People visiting the forest do not realize that there are other ghosts in the park. In one case, a Boy Scout troop found a large mound of stones that appeared to have been a makeshift grave. No one was willing to find out, but it does speak to a natural understanding of humans to see stone outcroppings that might not be natural and could have been created by man for the purpose of something else. Another ghost is that of the grave of Robert A. Taylor, who died in 1937. This grave is located in the park in the area known as the Taylor Farmstead. This lone stone is a reminder of the family who once lived where the national forest is today.

The ghosts of forest trails are easy to live with, but the ghost of the racial divide that once and still exists is being discussed. On May 7 and 8, 2016, members of the Slave Dwelling project spent two nights at the Brentsville

Jail. While they were not looking for ghosts in the spooky sense, they did discover ghosts of a different kind. What they found were the fingerprints of past prisoners in the jail, some of whom were African American, and evidence that corroborated many of the stories surrounding a number of African American experiences in the jail during the 1800s.

What truly irked members of the project was how people immediately gravitated toward the ghostly experiences of the African American prisoners as compared to information on their lives and why their imprisonment occurred. Sharon Williams, a member of the group who spent the night at Brentsville, stated that she was told by fellow overnight guest Joe McGill that a person could learn more about African American history through ghost stories than anywhere else. While the quote makes McGill look as though he was whitewashing history, there is an argument that can show the exact opposite. By focusing ghost stories on specific groups of people (in this case the African American community), it makes the audience more interested in the history of the true story.

An example of this argument comes from the story of Agness, who was mentioned in chapter 4. Agness was put on trial for murdering her master and was sentenced to death by hanging. The Virginia General Assembly had passed a law dictating that white people being prosecuted of capital crimes had to be tried in Richmond, while black people could be tried in their local jurisdictions, so the Brentsville Courthouse sentenced more black people to hanging than white people. The case of Agness being found guilty and hanged had one extra detail that has been greatly overlooked in the past: Agness was pregnant. This meant that two people were going to be killed instead of one. The question of why the jury in Brentsville allowed this particular punishment to go forward provides an opportunity for historians to delve deeper into understanding African American history in Prince William County in the early nineteenth century.

While a number of historians try to right the wrong of turning history into a sideshow, archaeologists make discoveries that resurrect spirits of the past in different ways. The Manassas Battlefield recently discovered a mass grave of limbs from soldiers who were horribly wounded during the First and Second Battles of Manassas. These grisly reminders of the horrors of war make people wonder whether these remains could be the physical remnants of the ghosts who supposedly haunt the battlefield.

In addition to the lost limbs of soldiers who fought on the battlefield, archaeologists have also been able to discover lost graves and tombstones throughout the county. In the case of lost graves, the Dumfries Cemetery

The tombstone of an unknown child buried in the Dumfries Cemetery. *Author's collection.*

is home to the unmarked grave of an infant. After reburying the infant, the Dumfries community placed a new stone over the grave of this child so that people knew of its existence.

As for forgotten tombstones, two large tombstones took a long, unique journey to make their way to Rippon Lodge. The first is that of Martin Scarlit, who died in 1695. His stone was pulled from the Occoquan River and placed in a wildlife refuge but was eventually placed in Rippon Lodge's cemetery in 2005. The second stone was also pulled from the Occoquan River but has very few words left on it. These two markers are reminders of those early inhabitants of the area who hacked their way through the wilderness and started to lay the foundations of a community.

While the foundations of the county might not have been immortalized with many monuments, the events of the Civil War that occurred in Prince William County certainly have. On July 21, 1911, one thousand veterans of the war from both the Union and the Confederacy came to the Manassas Battlefield for a ceremonial shaking of hands to celebrate peace and reunion. Four years later, a Peace Jubilee Monument was erected on the courthouse lawn in Manassas. The monument consisted of a plaque commemorating the event, two four-hundred-pound anchors (sent by then assistant secretary of the navy and future president of the United States Franklin D. Roosevelt) and two cannons flanking the anchors. Although the monument remains erected today, the recent turn of public attention toward removing symbols of the Confederacy could eventually bring it down.

Left: The tombstone of Martin Scarlit, whose grave is long lost. His stone is still visited at Rippon Lodge's cemetery. *Library of Congress.*

Right: The well-worn tombstone of an early resident of Prince William County, now located at Rippon Lodge's cemetery. *Author's collection.*

Even with certain negative aspects of Prince William County's history, there is still an appeal to ghost stories found in the county. "It is a good thing for tourism," said Ann Marie Maher, director of Discover Prince William and Manassas. Her office has worked tirelessly to get paranormal enthusiasts to come to Prince William County to create interest in ghost stories, ghost hunting and other activities that help bring revenue into the county. Every October, the county comes alive with different ghostly activities designed to entertain both the young and old with aspects of the macabre and the possibility of encountering a ghost.

With all of the interest in ghosts and their existence, there is one particular thought that does raise an interesting question: what if there are ghosts all around us, but people do not realize it? Does this mean people do not care about the true history these ghost stories represent?

In 1987, the *Potomac News* interviewed Cecil Garrison, a ninety-two-year-old resident of Prince William County who knew a great deal of information about ghosts in the county. In his own words, Garrison said he had seen many

The Tebbs House as seen before it was dismantled and sent to Fredericksburg. *Library of Congress.*

ghosts in his youth. One location that reportedly had ghosts was the old Tebbs House in Dumfries. As Garrison recalled, the ghosts did not have any heads and did not make much noise. Instead, it was Garrison and his friends who would make most of the noise in the house. Interestingly enough, one of the final photographs of the Tebbs House has written on it that the home was haunted. Sadly, the building no longer exists, as it was torn down, and the bricks of the structure were moved to Fredericksburg. "Bob King took all the bricks to Fredericksburg and the ghosts went away," said Garrison. "All the ghosts went to Fredericksburg."

Cecil Garrison was asked if he believed in ghosts. His response was, "No. Well, I used to when I was a boy." He went on to explain how people who once believed in ghosts stopped after a certain point. The reason for this change in belief seemed to be from the fact that as people become smarter, they stop believing in superstitious things. This particular point of view does have a certain degree of truth in it. If we become too smart to believe in ghosts, then do they actually exist? Even more frightening, what happens if there is no one around to tell us about these long-lost and forgotten spirits?

As the older generations passed away, those who were left behind did not always take the time to record the knowledge and the experiences of their elders while they were still alive. As a result of this, the ghost of lost knowledge becomes ever present. While researching this book, the number of people I spoke with who did not know anything about ghosts, despite claiming to have lived in Prince William County for a long time, was staggering. With this lack of knowledge, it creates a pitfall where researchers may come to a premature conclusion that the topics they are researching may not have any substance because no one knows the first thing about them. As a result, the last words Cecil Garrison had for the *Potomac News* held even more weight than he might have realized as he lamented, "These young people don't know a thing about ghosts."

BIBLIOGRAPHY

Books

Brown, Beth. *Haunted Battlefields: Virginia's Civil War Ghosts.* Atglen, PA: Schiffer Publishing, 2008.

Brown, George. *A History of Prince William County.* Prince William, VA: Prince William County Historical Commission, 2006.

Colman, Penny. *Corpses, Coffins, and Crypts: A History of Burial.* New York: Henry Holt, 1997.

Curtis, Donald E. *The Curtis Collection: A Personal View of Prince William County History.* Prince William, VA: Prince William County Historical Commission, 2006.

Prince William County and Manassas Convention and Visitors Bureau. *Prince William County.* Charleston, SC: Arcadia Publishing, 2007.

Puckle, Bertram S. *Funeral Customs: Their Origin and Development.* London: Werner Laurie, 1926.

Scheel, Eugene M. *Crossroads and Corners: A Tour of the Villages, Towns, and Post Offices of Prince William County, Virginia Past and Present.* Prince William, VA: Historic Prince William, 1996.

Taylor, L.B. *Civil War Ghosts of Virginia.* 12 vols. Williamsburg, VA: Progress Printing Company, 1995–2008.

Virginia Writers' Project. *Prince William: The Story of Its People and Its Places.* Manassas, VA: Bethlehem Club, 1988.

Wieder, Laurie C. *Prince William: A Past to Preserve.* Prince William, VA: Prince William County Historical Commission, 1998.

Articles

Broadus, Jade. "Scary Ghost Tours at Weems-Botts Museum in Dumfries, Virginia." October 9, 2013. inspiration.travel mindset.com.

Brown, George. "The Indians and the Collision of Cultures." 1991. www.historicprincewilliam.org.

Colgan, Chris. "Haunted Places in Prince William County." Active Rain. https://activerain.com

———. "Is the Olde Towne Inn in Manassas Really Haunted." Colgan Team. October 10, 2015. https://www.colganrealestate.com.

"Ghosts March Through Time at Battlefield, Legend Says." *Washington Post*, October 26, 1989.

Hunley, Jonathan. "In Manassas, a Ghost Tale of Flames, Luck, and Paranormal Profit." *Washington Post*, October 30, 2016.

Hunter, Kira. "These Local Venues Have a History of Hauntings." *Northern Virginia Magazine*, October 10, 2017.

"Korns, Hoops and Claws. An Unmannerly Ghost Wakes up the People in Prince William County." *Memphis Daily Avalanche*, December 25, 1868.

May, Michelle. "Ghostly Residents Linger." *Potomac News*, October 29, 1987.

McGill, Joe. "Sorry to Disappoint: The Brentsville Jail." Slave Dwelling Project. May 28, 2016. slavedwellingproject.org.

Morton, Susan Rogers. "Thorough Gap and Environs." Works Progress Administration of Virginia Historical Inventory. August 6, 1937.

Newman, Chris. "Some Say Spirit Opens, Closes Door." *Manassas Journal Messenger*, October 31, 2000.

Nolan, Jim. "Kaine: 'Old Virginny Is Dead.'" *Richmond Times Dispatch*, November 5, 2008.

Pirok, Alena. "Ghosts in the Archives: Communing with the Virginia Historical Inventory." October 18, 2017. www.virginiamemory.com.

Potomac Local News. "Explore These Ghostly Haunts of Prince William County." October 18, 2016. potomaclocal.com.

———. "Fighting Injustice with Injustice—Rippon Lodge's Tale of Woe." October 4, 2018. potomaclocal.com.

———. "The Five Creepiest Places to Visit in Prince William County." October 12, 2017. potomaclocal.com.

Pugh, Kari. "Rippon Lodge: 'Ghostly and Sinister.'" Inside NOVA. October 31, 2014. www.insidenova.com.

Ross, Bobby, Jr. "The Ghost of Prince William County." November 8, 2012. www.patheos.com.

Ruane, Michael E. "Bones of Civil War Dead Tell Their Horror Stories." *Times Union*, June 20, 2018.

Streng, Aileen. "One of Virginia's Most Haunted Places to Appear on Travel Channel Show." May 25, 2017. www.fauquier.com.

Tipple, Stephanie. "Civil War Soldiers Never Left Stone House." Potomac Local News. October 9, 2012. potomaclocal.com.

————. "A Dumfries House Full of History, and Chilling Experiences." Potomac Local News. October 31, 2012.

"A Virginia Ghost Is It the Devil?" *Pomeroy's Democrat*, January 20, 1869.

Walker, Keith. "Ghost Hunters Team Pays Visit to Brentsville." *Times Dispatch*, August 15, 2009.

Websites

Belanger, Jeff, and Frank Grace. Abandoned Haunts. ghostvillage.com.

Historic Occoquan, Virginia. historicoccoquan.com.

Lynn, Carolyn. *Prince William County Genealogy* (blog). pwcogenealogy. blogspot.com.

National Park Service. nps.gov.

Penot, Jessica. *Haunting Darkness* (blog). ghoststoriesandhauntedplaces. blogspot.com.

Riddle, Aaron. *Rockledge Mansion Photography* (blog). rockledgemansion.com.

The Winery at La Grange. wineryatlagrange.com

About the Author

Born and raised in Prince William County, Andrew Mills is a historian who is always looking for amazing stories from the past. By focusing on making history interesting, exciting and accessible, Andrew enjoys sharing his knowledge with everyone he meets. For eleven years, Andrew worked as a tour guide with Alexandria Colonial Tours, where he was able to learn about ghost stories in Northern Virginia and gain the necessary foundation to branch out and research these stories on his own. In addition, Andrew helps interpret George Washington's Mount Vernon, reenacts at Rippon Lodge and provides historical insight for visitors coming to the Northern Virginia area.

Having been featured on Destination America and C-SPAN, Andrew continues his work on television with his program *Virginia Time Travel*, which has been airing episodes since 2006. In addition to television, Andrew has written a number of books, including *Alexandria 1861–1865* (co-authored with Charles A. Mills), *The Washington Heir*, *The Female Stranger* and *The Stolen Sash*.

Currently, Andrew lives in Prince William County with his family surrounded by numerous haunted locations. While none of the spirits come to his house and visit him, he does enjoy going out and visiting them at their homes.